OLD WESTMORELAND

A History of Western Pennsylvania
During the Revolution

Edgar Wakefield Hassler

HERITAGE BOOKS
2007

HERITAGE BOOKS
AN IMPRINT OF HERITAGE BOOKS, INC.

Books, CDs, and more—Worldwide

For our listing of thousands of titles see our website
at
www.HeritageBooks.com

A Facsimile Reprint
Published 2007 by
HERITAGE BOOKS, INC.
Publishing Division
65 East Main Street
Westminster, Maryland 21157-5026

Copyright © 1900 Edgar Wakefield Hassler

— Publisher's Notice —
In reprints such as this, it is often not possible to remove blemishes from the original. We feel the contents of this book warrant its reissue despite these blemishes and hope you will agree and read it with pleasure.

International Standard Book Number: 978-0-7884-1027-7

CONTENTS.

CHAPTER I.

OLD WESTMORELAND.—Its Erection as a County.—Boundaries and Area.—Sources of Settlement.—Territorial Conflict with Virginia.—Early Centers of Population.—The Men of Ulster.—Pittsburg.—Leaders Among the Pioneers.................................5-10

CHAPTER II.

THE OUTBREAK OF REVOLUTION.—Delegates Sent to the Provincial Convention of 1774.—Sympathy with Boston.—Royalist Efforts of John Connolly.—Patriot Meeting at Pittsburg.—Association of Westmoreland Formed at Hannastown.—Military Organization.—The Rattlesnake Flag.—Ft. Pitt Occupied by Virginia Militia..11-17

CHAPTER III.

WILLIAM WILSON'S INDIAN TOUR.—The Savage Menace to the Frontier.—Ft. Pitt Treaty in October, 1775.—Iroquois Hostility.—George Morgan, Indian Agent.—Wilson Sent as a Peace Messenger to the Ohio Tribes.—His Peril at Pluggystown.—Before Governor Hamilton at Detroit.—The Unavailing Treaty at Ft. Pitt, October, 1776..18-23

CHAPTER IV.

CAPTURE OF ANDREW MCFARLANE.—First Indian Depredations.—McFarlane's History.—A Prisoner of the Virginians.—Love Romance and Marriage.—A Trader at Kittanning.—Without Military Protection.—The Tradition of the Lewis Family.—McFarlane Taken Prisoner.—His Captivity and Release.......................24-30

CHAPTER. V.

GIBSON'S POWDER EXPLOIT.—Scarcity of Ammunition on the Frontier.—George Gibson and William Linn.—The Lambs.—Journey to New Orleans.—Oliver Pollock.—Gibson in a Spanish Prison.—Return by Sea and River...................................31-36

CHAPTER VI.

THE SQUAW CAMPAIGN.—Congress Takes Charge of the Frontier Defense.—Brigadier General Edward Hand Appointed Commandant at Ft. Pitt.—Indian Raiders from Detroit.—Depredations in Westmoreland.—Expedition Up the Mahoning Valley.—Hand's Disappointment and Resignation................................37-43

CHAPTER VII.

FLIGHT OF THE PITTSBURG TORIES.—British Agents in Western Pennsylvania.—Captain Alexander McKee.—Matthew Elliott.—Escape from McKees Rocks.—Simon Girty.—Renegades in Coshocton.—Baffled by White Eyes.—Welcomed at Detroit.—Traitors in the Ft. Pitt Garrison.—Their Flight, Recapture and Punishment...44-48

(iii)

CHAPTER VIII.

THE TORIES OF SINKING VALLEY.—The Spy Among the Mountaineers.—Conspiracy for Murder and Spoliation.—John Weston.—Panic on the Juniata.—The Flight to Kittanning.—Fate of the Tory Leader.—Dispersal of the Plotters........................49-53

CHAPTER IX.

FATAL VOYAGE OF DAVID RODGERS.—Second Effort to Procure Powder from the Spaniards.—Captain David Rodgers.—His Redstone Company.—Time Lost on the Mississippi.—The Surprise at the Licking River.—Rodgers Mortally Wounded.—Singular Experience of Robert Benham and Basil Brown........................54-59

CHAPTER X.

THE EIGHTH PENNSYLVANIA.—Brigadier General Lachlan McIntosh ordered to Ft. Pitt.—His Two Border Regiments.—Mackay's Battalion.—The Winter March Over the Mountains.—Fatalities Among Officers and Privates.—Daniel Brodhead Colonel.—Morgan's Rifle Corps.—Thirteenth Virginia........................60-66

CHAPTER XI.

BACK TO THE HARRIED FRONTIER.—March of the Regulars for Ft. Pitt.—The Big Runaway.—The Massacre of Wyoming.—Eighth Pennsylvania Sent Up the Susquehanna.—Captain John Brady's Fort at Muncy.—The Killing of James Brady.—Samuel Brady, the Rifleman.—The Eighth at Ft. Pitt........................67-72

CHAPTER XII.

THE ALLIANCE WITH THE DELAWARES.—McIntosh's Design Against Detroit.—Seeking Indian Allies.—The Ft. Pitt Treaty with the Delawares.—White Eyes.—Proposal for an Indian State....73-79

CHAPTER XIII.

FORT LAURENS.—McIntosh Advances Westward.—Ft. McIntosh.—Death of White Eyes.—Building of Ft. Laurens.—A Winter in the Wilderness.—Colonel Gibson Besieged.—Captain Bird and Simon Girty.—Ft. Laurens Relieved.—Resignation of McIntosh.—Colonel Brodhead in Command.—Ft. Laurens Deserted...............80-87

CHAPTER XIV.

SAMUEL BRADY'S REVENGE.—Incursions from the North.—Military Scouts.—Brady Hears of His Father's Death.—Attack on Ft. Hand.—Raid on the Sewickley Settlement.—Brady on the Trail.—Indians Surprised in their Camp.—Death of the Muncy Captain. 88-94

CHAPTER XV.

BRODHEAD'S RAID UP THE ALLEGHENY.—The Hostile Senecas.—Sullivan's Expedition.—Brodhead's Co-operation.—Difficult March Up the Allegheny.—Fight with the Indians.—Devastation of Seneca Cornfields.—Muncy Village Destroyed.—Return by the Venango Path.—Thanks of Congress........................95-101

CONTENTS. v

CHAPTER XVI.

THE WINTER OF THE DEEP SNOW.—Influence of Weather on the Frontier.—Severest Winter on Record.—Suffering of Soldiers.—Animals and Birds Killed.—Raids in the Ohio River Settlements by Western Indians.—Rewards for Scalps and Prisoners.—Brady's Daring Journey to the Sandusky.—Rescue of Mrs. Stoops..... 102-108

CHAPTER XVII.

THE SUMMER OF THE BIG HARVEST.—Great Crops of Wheat and Corn, but no Water for the Mills.—Cattle Scarce.—Money Depreciation.—Agitation for a New State.—Soldiers Suffer for Food.—On the Verge of Mutiny.—Brady Sent Out to Impress Live Stock.—Futile Efforts to Organize an Expedition Into the Indian Country.—Buffaloes for Food... 109-115

CHAPTER XVIII.

THE DERRY SETTLEMENT.—A Typical Ulster Population and Its Leaders.—The Three Forts.—Major Campbell and Companions Captured on Blacklick.—The Unsolved Fate of Lieutenant Craig.—Attack on Ft. Wallace.—Retaliation by the Borderers.—Defeat of Captain Hopkins.—Escape of Ebenezer Finley.—Major Wilson's Combat Near Ft. Wallace.—John Pomeroy's Defense of His Cabin..116-122

CHAPTER XIX.

THE DESTRUCTION OF COSHOCTON.—Delawares Join the Hostile League.—Chief Killbuck Ostracized.—Brodhead's Expedition.—Rendezvous at Wheeling.—Indian Capital Surprised.—Assault in the Rain.—Warriors Killed.—Coshocton Plundered and Burned.—Kindness of the Moravians.—Chief Killbuck's Stroke.—The Misrepresentations of Doddridge.—Migration of the Delawares.......... 123-130

CHAPTER XX.

GENERAL CLARK'S DRAFT.—Design Against Detroit.—Buying Provisions.—George Rogers Clark in Western Pennsylvania.—Raising Volunteers.—Factions Among the Settlers.—Official Approval.—Help from the Westmoreland Militia.—Erection of Washington County.—Efforts to Enforce the Draft.—Pillage and Personal Violence.—Small Force Assembled.—Clark Discouraged but Persistent.—Failure of His Expedition.. 131-138

CHAPTER XXI.

LOCHRY'S DISASTER.—Westmoreland Detachment to Aid Clark.—Rendezvous at Carnaghan's.—March to Wheeling.—Left Behind by the Main Body.—Slow Journey Down the Ohio.—Loss of Captain Shannon.—Ambush at Lochry's Run.—Joseph Brant and His Mohawks.—Killing of Lochry.—Entire Party Slain or Taken....139-145

CHAPTER XXII.

MORAVIANS AND WYANDOTS.—Lochry Succeeded as County Lieutenant by Edward Cook.—Charges Against Brodhead.—Ordered by Washington to Resign.—His Successor Brigadier General William Irvine.—Moravian Missions on the Tuscarawas Broken Up by British and Indians.—Privations of the Red Converts.—Sons of the Half-King Raid Washington County.—Adventure of the Poe Brothers 146-152

CHAPTER XXIII.

The Slaughter at Gnadenhuetten.—Williamson's First Visit to the Tuscarawas.—Indian Towns Deserted.—Washington County Raided.—Mrs. Wallace and Her Children Captured.—The Escape and Revelations of John Carpenter.—Williamson's Second Campaign to the Tuscarawas.—Mutilated Corpses Beside the Trail.—Rage of the Frontiersmen.—Moravian's Surprised Gathering Corn.—Telltale Trophies.—The Vote for Life or Death.—Condemnation.—Massacre of the Guilty and the Innocent.—Indian Villages Burned.—The Raid on Smoky Island.—Investigation Thwarted.................153-161

CHAPTER XXIV.

Crawford's Expedition and Death.—Plans for the Destruction of Wyandot Towns on the Sandusky.—Aid from General Irvine.—Muster at Mingo.—Crawford Chosen to Command.—His Staff and Captains.—March Into the Wilderness.—Enemy Forewarned.—Battle on Sandusky Plain.—Night Retreat and Panic.—Crawford's Capture.—Williamson's Retreat.—Crawford and Others Burned at the Stake...162-169

CHAPTER XXV.

The Wounded Indian.—Attack on Walthour's Station.—Killing of Willard and Daughter.—The Lame Delaware at Pittsburg.—His Confession.—Clamor of the Settlers for His Death.—Davy Delivered Up.—His Escape from the Blockhouse.—The Gray Mare.—Never Reached Home..170-175

CHAPTER XXVI.

The Destruction of Hannastown.—Savage Inroad from the Seneca Land.—Guyasuta.—Escape of the Harvesters.—Refuge in the Stockade.—Assault Repelled.—Death of Margaret Shaw.—Burning of the Town.—Raid on Miller's Station.—Killing of Lieutenant Brownlee and Others.—The End of Hannastown..................176-181

CHAPTER XXVII.

The Abandoned Expedition.—Planning Another Campaign Against Sandusky.—General Irvine to Command.—Approved by Government.—Attack on Wheeling.—Gallant Defense of Rice's Blockhouse.—Savages Called Off by General Carleton.—Expedition Countermanded by General Washington.—Clark's Raid on the Shawnee Towns.—General Thanksgiving Day..................182-188

CHAPTER XXVIII.

The Peace Journey of Ephraim Douglass.—Isolated Depredations in Washington County.—Appeal to Congress.—Douglass Commissioned.—His Journey to Sandusky.—Before DePeyster at Detroit.—Douglass Sent to Niagara.—Talk with Joseph Brant.—End of the Border War...189-194

LIST OF AUTHORITIES.

American Archives, edited by Peter Force, 9v., 1837-53.
Annals of the West, James R. Albach, Pittsburg, 1856.
Calendar of Virginia State Papers, Richmond, 1875.
Chronicles of Border Warfare, A. S. Withers, Cincinnati, 1895.
Colonial Records of Pennsylvania, Published by the State, 16v., 1851-3.
Conquering the Wilderness, Frank Triplett, New York, 1883.
Diary of David McClure, New York, 1899.
Fort McIntosh, Its Times and Men, Daniel Agnew, 1893.
Fort Pitt and Letters from the Frontier, edited by Mrs. M. C. O'H. Darlington, Pittsburg, 1892.
Frontier Forts of Pennsylvania, Published by the State, 2v., Harrisburg, 1896.
Historical Account of the Expedition Against Sandusky, C. W. Butterfield, Cincinnati, 1873.
Historical Collections of Ohio, Henry Howe, revised edition, Norwalk, O., 1896.
Historical Collections of the State of Pennsylvania, Sherman Day, Philadelphia, 1843.
Historical Register, Published Monthly in Pittsburg, 1883-4.
History, Manners and Customs of the Indian Natives, etc., John Heckewelder, Philadelphia, 1818.
History of Allegheny County, Published by Warner & Co., Chicago, 1890.
History of Huntingdon County, Pa., M. S. Lytle, Lancaster, Pa., 1876.
History of Indiana County, Pa., Caldwell.
History of Ohio, James W. Taylor, Cincinnati, 1854.
History of Pennsylvania, W. H. Egle, Harrisburg, 1876.
History of Pittsburg, N. B. Craig, Pittsburg, 1851.
History of the Juniata Valley, U. J. Jones, Philadelphia, 1856.
History of the Missions of the United Brethren, George Henry Loskiel, London, 1794.
History of Washington County, Pa., Boyd Crumrine, Philadelphia, 1882.
History of Westmoreland County, edited by G. Dallas Albert, 1882.
Indian Tribes of the United States, H. R. Schoolcraft, Published by Congress, 1851-5.

(i)

Journal of Two Visits, etc., Rev. David Jones, New York, 1865.
Magazine of American History.
Memoirs of John Bannister Gibson, Thomas P. Roberts, Pittsburg, 1890.
Memoirs of the Historical Society of Pennsylvania.
Monongahela of Old, James Veech, Pittsburg, 1852-1892.
Narrative of the Mission of the United Brethren, John Heckewelder, Philadelphia, 1820.
Notes and Queries, W. H. Egle, Harrisburg.
Notes on the Settlements and Indian Wars, etc., Joseph Doddridge, revised edition, 1876.
Olden Time, edited by N. B. Craig, Pittsburg, 1846-8.
Old Redstone, Rev. Joseph Smith, Philadelphia, 1854.
Otzinachson, or a History of the West Branch Valley, John F. Meginness, 1857.
Our Western Border, Charles McKnight, Pittsburg, 1875.
Pennsylvania Archives, First Series, Published by the State, 12v., 1852-6.
Pennsylvania Archives, Second Series, Published by the State, 20v., 1875-90.
Pennsylvania Magazine of History and Biography.
Pioneer History, Samuel P. Hildreth, Cincinnati, 1848.
Romance of Western History, James Hall, Cincinnati, 1885.
St. Clair Papers, edited by W. H. Smith, Cincinnati, 1882.
The Girtys, C. W. Butterfield, Cincinnati, 1890.
Three Villages (Gnadenhuetten), William Dean Howells, Boston, 1884.
Washington-Crawford Letters, C. W. Butterfield, Cincinnati, 1877.
Washington-Irvine Correspondence, C. W. Butterfield, Madison, Wis., 1882.
Washington's Letters to the American Congress, New York, 1796.
Westward Movement, Justin Winsor, Boston, 1897.
Winning of the West, Theodore Roosevelt, New York, 1889.
Writings of George Washington, P. L. Ford, New York, 1889.

PREFACE.

This book represents an effort to tell the revolutionary history of the Western Pennsylvania border; to describe the trials, the sacrifices, the errors and the heroisms of the frontiersmen, in their conflicts with tories, British partisans and savages, during the years when Washington and his generals were fighting for independence along the Atlantic seaboard. The American Revolution covered many fields of action, and the operations on each contributed to the grand result. The men who defended the western border against the savage tribes were doing their work essential to the cause of freedom as well as the ragged Continentals who faced British and Hessian battalions in New York or New Jersey.

Naturally the operations in the East, where the main conflict raged and the issue was decided, have received the chief attention of historians; but the struggles on the western frontier have been unduly neglected. Some attention has been given to the revolutionary history of the New York and Tennessee frontiers, but no book tells, in connected form, of the important operations in that great transmontane region of which Ft. Pitt was the center, during the years from 1775 to 1783.

Many volumes of border history have been published but none of them has been devoted to this period. Most of them are out of print or beyond the reach of the average reader. Those that have enjoyed the greatest popularity have been collections of frontier adventures, based chiefly on unreliable traditions, marvelous and often absurd, in many cases disproven by contemporary records made public in recent years.

I have tried, by a study of the original records, to find the facts and to set them forth in plain, condensed and impartial form. The tale is sufficiently interesting and more instructive without the embellishments of fiction.

A prime object of this publication is to stimulate a local interest in pioneer history. It is good for those who participate in the wondrous industrial development of Western Pennsylvania and Eastern Ohio to know how this fertile region was won and held from savagery.

The inhabitants of Pittsburg and its neighborhood who feel an inclination to study the early times, enjoy, at the present day, facilities which were beyond their reach only half a dozen years ago. These facilities have come through the establishment and rapid up-building of the Carnegie Library of Pittsburg. Without that institution this work could not have been written in Western Pennsylvania. The library already contains almost every book and pamphlet that has been published, within 130 years, bearing on our pioneer history. Many of these works are extremely rare and valuable, but they are now within the reach of all. The library contains all the authorities quoted in this volume, so that any reader who may desire to investigate for himself will find ample opportunity.

EDGAR W. HASSLER.

Pittsburg, Pa., May 1, 1900.

OLD WESTMORELAND.

CHAPTER I.

OLD WESTMORELAND.

The County of Westmoreland was erected by the Assembly of the Province of Pennsylvania by an act signed by Lieutenant Governor Richard Penn, on Friday, February 26, 1773. It was the eleventh county of the Commonwealth and the last erected under the proprietary government. Like all the earlier counties of Pennsylvania, except Philadelphia, it received its name from a county in England. This name, as applied to the most distant territory of the Province, was especially appropriate.

The land comprised in the new county was bought by the Penns from the Six Nations or Iroquois Indians, at a treaty held at Fort Stanwix, N. Y., in November, 1768, and was opened for settlement in the following April. Its northern boundary was a line extending from Canoe Point, on the West Branch of the Susquehanna river, west by north to the site of the Indian town called Kittanning, on the Allegheny river, thence down along the Allegheny and the Ohio rivers to the western limit of the Province, while its western and southern lines were to be the western and southern boundaries of Pennsylvania, not yet definitely ascertained. In 1771 this wide region was included in the county of Bedford, but settlements grew so rapidly west of the mountains during the year 1772 that a new frontier county was soon demanded. The evacuation of Fort Pitt by the British troops, in the fall of 1772, also led the borderers to demand a stronger civil organization.

When Westmoreland was erected it covered all of the Province west of the Laurel Hill, being what is broadly known as Southwestern Pennsylvania. In included the present counties of Westmoreland, Fayette, Greene and Washington, the parts of Allegheny and Beaver counties south of the Ohio river, about two-thirds of the county of Indiana and one-third of the county of Armstrong, the total area being about 4,700 square miles.

While this was the area of Westmoreland in theory, it was restricted in fact by Virginia's seizure and government of a large portion of the territory. After the capture of Fort Duquesne from the French in 1758 and the construction of Fort Pitt in the following year, a few settlements were made along the Forbes and Braddock roads, by permission of the Fort Pitt commandant. These permissions were granted to tavern keepers, that they might give shelter and entertainment to persons traveling on the king's business.[1] The general settlement of the country west of the Alleghany Mountains did not begin until the Pennsylvania land office was opened for the granting of warrants, in the spring of 1769.

Population flowed into the new region through two channels. Scots from the Cumberland Valley and other settled parts of the Province made their way westward by the Forbes military road and planted their cabins along its course, from the lovely Ligonier Valley to Fort Pitt. These men were faithful to Pennsylvania, under whose seal they held their lands. From the Valley of Virginia other Scots crossed the mountains by way of the old Braddock road and occupied the rich lands along the Monongahela and Youghiogheny rivers and Chartiers creek. These men were Virginians and believed that their settlements

---

[1] Calendar of Virginia State Papers, Richmond, 1875, vol. i., under date of March 10, 1777.

were still within the territory of the Old Dominion. It had not yet been determined by survey how far Pennsylvania extended westward of the mountains. Virginia claimed all the interior country west of Pennsylvania and asserted that the entire valley of the Monongahela, including Pittsburg, was within her jurisdiction.

A lively contest for the control of the region tributary to Pittsburg began between Pennsylvania and Virginia. The organization of Westmoreland county was designed to strengthen the Pennsylvania authority, and sixteen magistrates were appointed to administer justice within its boundaries. The county seat was established at Robert Hanna's little settlement on the Forbes road, 35 miles east of Pittsburg, and at Hannastown the first Pennsylvania court west of the mountains was held in April, 1773. These proceedings stirred up the Virginia authorities. The Earl of Dunmore, governor of Virginia, took forcible possession of the disputed territory. He appointed John Connolly, of Pittsburg "captain commandant of Pittsburg and its dependencies." Connolly mustered the militia under Virginia law, seized and garrisoned Fort Pitt, intimidated the Pennsylvania magistrates, marched some of them off to prison, and established the authority of Virginia throughout all the region between the Monongahela and the Ohio. Pennsylvania, having no militia law, was powerless to resist this usurpation.[2]

Thus it came about that, during the Revolution, the authority of Westmoreland county was limited to about half of its actual area. It was not until the summer of 1780 that Virginia agreed to accept the results of a joint survey which would extend the southern boundary line of Pennsylvania (Mason and Dixon's line) to a distance of five degrees of longitude west of the Delaware river. This joint survey was delayed, by official quibbling and the hostility of the Virginia settlers, until the fall of 1782. In the the spring of 1781 that part of Westmoreland lying west of

---

2 See St. Clair Papers, Cincinnati, 1882, vol. i.; and Force's American Archives, vol. i., many letters under date of 1774.

the Monongahela was set off as a new county, named Washington, so that the officers of Westmoreland never had the privilege of exercising their authority over the whole extent of their large territory.

In 1775 the Ligonier Valley, extending along the eastern border of the county, was well settled. The focus of settlement was the village of Ligonier, where a British fort had been built in 1758, and the principal man was Captain Arthur St. Clair, a Scotchman who had served under Wolf at Quebec and had afterward become the agent of the Penn family in Western Pennsylvania.[3] West of the Chestnut Ridge, along Loyalhanna and its little tributaries, settlements were rather numerous as far as Hannastown, on the Forbes road. To the north of the road, between the Loyalhanna and the Conemaugh, was the Derry settlement, so called from the city of Ireland whence most of its people came. Nearly all the pioneers in this eastern part of the county were Scots from Ulster, or their immediate descendants, with a slight sprinkling of Irish of Presbyterian faith. Another center of Ulster settlement was at the Braddock road crossing of Big Sewickley creek, a tributary of the Youghiogheny; while lower down on that creek and on Turtle and Brush creeks were the cabins and blockhouses of German emigrants from the Rhine Palatinate.

Among the Virginia settlers along the Youghiogheny and Monongahela rivers and westward to the Ohio there were not many natives of either Scotland or Ireland. The people were two or three generations removed from the old country, but nearly all were of Scotch stock. The larger land owners had brought their slaves with them from Virginia and negroes were held in bondage in Southwestern Pennsylvania until long after the Revolution.

At Pittsburg some of the principal characters, chiefly traders, were members of the Church of England, and it was among these men that the tory sentiment developed, during the Revolution. Old Westmoreland was, however, decidedly a Scotch and Calvinistic settlement. While the

---

3 St. Clair Papers, vol. i., p. 7.

territorial dispute between Pennsylvania and Virginia was very bitter, it was doubtless because the opposing forces consisted of men of the same race and creed that no homicides were committed during the long period of contention.

The Scotch pioneers of this western region were bold, stout and industrious men, sharp at bargains, fond of religious and political controversy and not strongly attached to government either of the royal or the proprietary kind. In nearly every cabin three articles were to be found: a Bible, a rifle and a whisky jug. A strong characteristic of the settlers was an intense hatred of the Indians, for whose treatment the extermination policy of Joshua toward the heathen beyond Jordan was generally considered to be the proper model.[4]

At the opening of the Revolution the village of Pittsburg was the largest center of population west of the mountains. When Washington visited the place in the autumn of 1770, he found about twenty log houses ranged along the Monongahela shore, "inhabited," he wrote in his journal, "by Indian traders."[5] During the succeeding four years emigration to the west was so heavy that by 1775 the town had probably trebled in size and the traders were no longer in the majority, although they formed the influential element. These traders were nearly all Pennsylvanians, but most of the other inhabitants were Virginians. With its taverns, its hard drinking traders, trappers and mule drivers, its fugitives from eastern justice and its frequent Indian visitors, Pittsburg was a rude and boisterous frontier settlement. Rev. David Jones, a Baptist missionary who visited the town in June, 1772, described it as "a small town chiefly inhabited by Indian traders and some mechanics. . . . Part of the inhabitants are agreeable and worthy of regard, while others are lamentably dissolute in their morals."[6]

---

4 Doddridge's Notes of the Settlements, etc.
5 The Writings of George Washington, P. L. Ford, New York, 1889, vol. ii., p. 290.
6 A Journal of Two Visits, etc., New York, 1865. See also the Diary of David McClure, New York, 1899, for an accurate account of social conditions at Pittsburg in 1772 and 1773.

The one man of most influence in this community was the fat old trader and Indian agent, Colonel George Croghan, who lived on a pretentious plantation about four miles up the Allegheny river. He was an Irishman by birth and an Episcopalian by religion, when he permitted religion to trouble him. He had long been a resident of Pennsylvania, but his landed interests attached him to Virginia. His nephew, Captain Connolly, who was the official representative of the Virginia government and a petty despot on the frontier, was under Croghan's guidance. Other leaders of the Virginia party on the border were John Campbell, a trader and land owner at Pittsburg; Dorsey Pentecost, who dwelt on a large estate called "Greenway" in the Forks of the Youghiogheny, and William Crawford, surveyor, land owner and agent for George Washington, living at Stewart's Crossing (now New Haven), on the Youghiogheny. Pentecost and Crawford were Virginians who had once held commissions as Pennsylvania magistrates but had later become violent partisans of the Virginia claims.

In 1775 the most prominent representative of the Pennsylvania interest in old Westmoreland was Captain Arthur St. Clair, at Ligonier; while others who took active parts were John Proctor and Archibald Lochry, living near the Forbes road west of Chestnut ridge; Robert Hanna and Michael Huffnagle, at Hannastown; James Cavet and Christopher Hays, of the Sewickley settlement; John Ormsby, Devereux Smith and Aeneas Mackay, traders and storekeepers at Pittsburg; Edward Cook, living in the Forks of the Youghiogheny a short distance below Redstone, and George Wilson, whose plantation was on the Monongahela at the mouth of George's creek, in the very heart of Virginianism.

CHAPTER II.

THE OUTBREAK OF REVOLUTION.

During 1774 the pioneers of Westmoreland were so occupied by their labor in clearing the forest, by the civil contention with Virginia and by the war between Virginia and the Shawnee Indians, that most of them heard little and thought little of the eastern agitation against the oppressions of the British Parliament. Yet scraps of news concerning the struggle going on in Boston occasionally reached the frontier and a few of the pioneers who had personal and official connection with Philadelphia kept in touch with the momentous contest then beginning with the mother country.

In May, 1774, on an appeal from Boston, a committee of correspondence was formed in Philadelphia. Under the date of June 12, a circular letter was addressed by this committee to certain of the principal inhabitants of the other counties in the Province, advising the formation of a similar committee in each county; and on June 28 the Philadelphia committee called a meeting of delegates from the several county committees. In response to this call, a "very respectable body of people"[1] met at Hannastown on Monday, July 11, and chose Robert Hanna and James Cavet to represent Westmoreland in the delegate convention. On July 15 this convention met in Philadelphia and its minutes show

---
[1] St. Clair Papers, vol. i., p. 325; American Archives, Fourth Series, vol. i., p. 549.

the presence of Hanna and Cavet. They could not have reached the provincial capital within four days after their election, but were doubtless in attendance before the meeting adjourned on July 21.[2]

This convention was not revolutionary. It expressly declared allegiance to King George, but denounced recent acts of the British Parliament, especially those for the closing of the port of Boston and the annulment of the Massachusetts charter, as unconstitutional. It approved a proposal for a colonial congress and pledged the readiness of the people of Pennsylvania to cease all commercial intercourse with Great Britain if necessary to secure a repeal of the obnoxious laws.

A fair inference from these proceedings is that a committee of correspondence was organized in Westmoreland in the early summer of 1774 and continued its existence until succeeded, a year later, by the revolutionary association. No records of this committee have been found. They were probably destroyed when the Indians burned Hannastown.

The American cause was, at the same time, arousing the sympathy of the leaders among the Virginia settlers in Southwestern Pennsylvania, although they were actively engaged in an Indian war. On October 1, 1774, while serving in Dunmore's army against the Shawnees, Valentine Crawford, brother of William Crawford, wrote from Wheeling to George Washington that the frontiersmen all hoped for an early peace with the savages, "in order that we may be able to assist you in relieving the poor distressed Bostonians. If the report here is true that General Gage has bombarded the city of Boston, this is a most alarming circumstance and calls on every friend of the liberty of his country to exert himself at this time in its cause."[3]

After the Shawnees had been forced to make peace in the valley of the Scioto river, the officers of Lord Dun-

---

[2] American Archives, Fourth Series, vol. i., p. 555.
[3] The Washington-Crawford Letters, Butterfield, Cincinnati, 1877, p. 99.

more's army, on the homeward march, held a meeting at the mouth of the Hocking river, on November 5, 1774, and unanimously declared their intention, as soldiers, to exert "every power within us for the defense of American liberty and for the support of our just rights and privileges."[4]

When it began to appear probable, early in 1775, that an armed conflict would occur between the colonies and the home government, Captain Connolly undertook to organize the chief men in Pittsburg and its neighborhood in the interest of Great Britain. He was of Irish-English blood, a member of the Church of England and a devout follower of the Earl of Dunmore. He wholly misapprehended the spirit of the Presbyterian Scots with whom he had been associated in the Virginia boundary contest. His efforts to seduce the pioneers from the American cause were almost entirely unavailing. They had stood by him in opposition to the territorial claims of the Penns, but when he sought to enlist them in opposition to the general colonial cause, they and he parted company.

The news of Lexington and Concord reached Pittsburg during the first week in May, 1775. To the liberty loving Scots and Irish of the frontier it was a signal to forget, for the time, their local jealousies and quarrels and to unite and organize in defense of their mutual rights as Americans. Pennsylvanians and Virginians joined hands to resist the hard enactments of the British Parliament. The committees of correspondence, one in eastern Westmoreland and the other in West Augusta, as the Virginians called the portion of the border which they controlled, at once called meetings of the settlers to declare their minds on the sudden crisis.

The Pittsburg meeting was held on Tuesday, May 16, being the day for the opening of the Virginia court in that village, and the attendance was large. The assembly chose a committee of 28 men, nearly all of whom are more or less famous in the border annals. Colonel George Croghan, who was afterward suspected of being lukewarm in the

---

[4] American Archives, Fourth Series, vol. i., p. 962.

American cause, was chairman, and other committeemen were Edward Ward, who surrendered the site of Fort Pitt to Contrecoeur in 1754; John Canon, the founder of Canonsburg; John McCulloch, a daring frontiersman; John Gibson, the interpreter of the celebrated speech of Logan the Mingo; Edward Cook, the founder of Cookstown, now Fayette City; William Crawford, the surveyor and land agent of Washington, and David Rodgers, a partisan leader who fell in combat with the Indians on the site of Newport, Ky. Of the 28 members of the body, at least five were Pennsylvania partisans in the territorial dispute. This committee adopted unanimously a resolution approving the acts of the New Englanders in resisting "the invaders of American rights and privileges to the utmost extreme," and formulated plans for the organization of military companies to be ready for the country's call.[5]

These proceedings gave great offense to Connolly and were a stinging personal rebuke to his royalist schemings. His uncle, Croghan, and his father-in-law, Samuel Semple, were members of the committee. Two days after the meeting Connolly sat for the last time as a member of the West Augusta court at Pittsburg, but for two months he remained in the settlement, endeavoring perseveringly to influence his acquaintances to support the royalist cause and plotting with Indian chiefs to make war on the colonists in the event of an actual revolution.[6]

On the day succeeding the meeting at Pittsburg, "a general meeting of the inhabitants of Westmoreland" was held in the log cabin settlement at Hannastown. Here also the action taken was distinctly revolutionary, for while the assembled borderers declared their allegiance to King George, they voted it to be the duty of every true American, "by every means which God has put in his power," to resist the oppression of the British Parliament and ministry, and they proceeded to form a military organization called the

---

5 Craig's History of Pittsburg, p. 128.
6 Connolly's Narrative, Pennsylvania Magazine of History and Biography, vol. xii., pp. 314-321.

THE OUTBREAK OF REVOLUTION. 15

Association of Westmoreland County, whose purpose was declared to be forcible resistance to the power of Great Britain.[7]

Captain St. Clair, who evidently took part in this meeting, was not in full sympathy with its radicalism. On May 18 he wrote to Joseph Shippen, Jr., the provincial secretary: "Yesterday we had a county meeting and have come to resolutions to arm and discipline, and have formed an association, which I suppose you will soon see in the papers. God grant an end may be speedily put to any necessity of such proceedings. I doubt their utility and am almost as much afraid of success in this contest as of being vanquished."[8]

In accordance with the Hannastown resolutions, meetings were held in every township one week later, on Wednesday, May 24, to form military companies. St. Clair wrote to Governor Penn on May 25: "We have nothing but musters and committees all over the country and everythings seems to be running into the wildest confusion. If some conciliating plan is not adopted by the congress, America has seen her golden days: they may return, but will be preceded by scenes of horror."

His forecast was correct. It was because the prospect of civil war appalled him that St. Clair doubted and held back at the outset. But he did not hesitate long. When he realized that the crisis could not be avoided, he earnestly devoted his life and his fortune to the patriot cause.

The yeomen of Westmoreland formed themselves into companies, elected their company officers and were arranged in two battalions. Of the first battalion the officers were: colonel, John Proctor, the first sheriff of the county; lieutenant colonel, Archibald Lochry; major, John Shields. The officers of the second battalion were: colonel, John Carnaghan, then sheriff; lieutenant colonel, Providence Mountz; major, James Smith, a famous character on the frontier, whose narrative of captivity among the Indians is one of

---

7 American Archives, Fourth Series, vol. ii., p. 615.
8 St. Clair Papers, vol. i., p. 353.

the interesting stories of the border.[9] It was Colonel Proctor's battalion which adopted as its banner the celebrated rattlesnake flag. It is of crimson silk, having, in the corner, on a blue field, the red and white crosses of St. George and St. Andrew. The emblems are worked in gold. Above a rattlesnake, coiled to strike, are the characters, "1. B. W. C. P.," meaning, First Battalion, Westmoreland County, Pennsylvania, and below the serpent is the motto, "Don't Tread on Me." Near the flag's upper margin is a monogram of J. P., the initials of John Proctor.

This flag was never carried into battle, but it was, doubtless, borne to Philadelphia when the battalion was called to the succor of that city at the beginning of 1777. The standard bearer was Lieutenant Samuel Craig, of the Derry settlement, and the silken relic is still carefully kept by his descendants in Westmoreland.

The tory conduct of Captain Connolly at Pittsburg became so bold and obnoxious that in June, 1775, he was seized by twenty men, under the orders of Captain St. Clair, and carried to Ligonier, with the intention of delivering him to the revolutionary government in Philadelphia. His arrest was misunderstood by many of the Virginia settlers, who thought it a blow at their territorial claims, and they made such violent demonstration that Captain St. Clair considered it advisable to let the prisoner go.[10] Soon after his release, Connolly fled from Pittsburg by night and made his way to Portsmouth, Va., where he joined Lord Dunmore on a man-of-war. From that refuge he continued his efforts, by correspondence, to influence border leaders in the king's cause and to stir up the Ohio tribes against the colonists.[11]

Some knowledge of Connolly's machinations and a fear of an Indian uprising persuaded the Virginia convention, in August, to direct Captain John Neville, a militia officer and a member of the patriot committee at Pittsburg,

---

9 Pennsylvania Archives, Second Series, vol. xiv., p. 675.
10 Connolly's Narrative, Pa. Mag. of Hist. and Biog., vol. xii., pp. 317-320; Washington-Crawford Letters, p. 102.
11 American Archives, Fourth Series, vol. iii., p. 72.

THE OUTBREAK OF REVOLUTION.

to occupy Fort Pitt with his company from the Shenandoah Valley. With about one hundred men, Captain Neville marched from Winchester and took possession of the fort on September 11.[12] He continued in command there until June 1, 1777, when he transferred the post to General Edward Hand, the representative of the United States of America. For a year and a half after the Revolution began the civil government of Western Pennsylvania was under the control of the two committees, one meeting at Hannastown and the other at Pittsburg, acting in conjunction with the justices of the peace who espoused the patriot cause; and this loose system of government continued until the autumn of 1776, when both Pennsylvania and Virginia had adopted state constitutions.

---

12 American Archives, Fourth Series, vol. iii., pp. 370, 376 and 717.

CHAPTER III.

WILLIAM WILSON'S INDIAN TOUR.

The men of the border did not feel themselves in danger from the British armies landed on the Atlantic coast, but from the beginning of the Revolution their homes and families were menaced by a more dreaded foe—the savage tribes of the wilderness. The quickly revealed plottings of Connolly at Ft. Pitt, to incite the Indians against the settlements, were believed to be a sample of what the British government would attempt on a general scale.

As early as July, 1775, the second Colonial Congress initiated measures to secure the friendship of the savages. The frontier was divided into three Indian departments, of which the middle department included the tribes west of Pennsylvania and Virginia, and three members of Congress, Benjamin Franklin and James Wilson, of Pennsylvania, and Patrick Henry, of Virginia, were appointed to hold a treaty with the Indians at Ft. Pitt.[1] This treaty was held in October, with a few chiefs of the Senecas, Delawares, Shawnees and Wyandots. Guyasuta was the principal Seneca chief in attendance, representing the Iroquois dwelling in the Allegheny valley and in the Ohio country. As an Iroquois, he assumed to speak for the western tribes, and thereby aroused White Eyes, the Delaware orator, to declare the absolute independence of the Delawares. The council was not harmonious, but the chiefs protested their

---

[1] American Archives, Fourth Series, vol. ii., pp. 1879, 1883.

intentions to remain neutral, and Guyasuta promised to use his influence with the great council of the Iroquois in New York, to obtain a decision in favor of peace.[2]

The Indians remained quiet during 1775 and the following winter, but it was not long until the agents of the British government outbid the colonists for a savage alliance. The British were able to give the greater bribes and to impress the savages with the greater display of military force. Sir Guy Johnson and Colonel John Butler held a great council with the Iroquois at Ft. Niagara, in May, 1776, when an overwhelming majority of the Iroquois voted to accept the war hatchet and to fight for the king.[3] That was the beginning of the mischief on the border. The influence of the Six Nations soon made itself manifest among the western tribes.

The Westmoreland settlers apprehended the storm long before it broke. They observed an alteration in the manner of the Indians with whom they came in frequent contact. In February, 1776, settlers near Pittsburg sent a memorial to Congress, complaining that Indian hunters were encroaching on the lands of the white people.[4] Van Swearingen, a pioneer of the Monongahela valley and one of the Pennsylvania magistrates, although a Virginian, raised a company of young riflemen and established a patrol along the Allegheny river.[5]

The Indian commissioners, at the treaty in October, 1775, selected John Gibson as Indian agent for the Ohio tribes. Gibson had intimate relations with the savages and was peculiarly adapted to the work, but had not sufficient influence at Philadelphia to retain his office. After a short term, he was succeeded by Richard Butler, another Pittsburg trader. In the spring of 1776 Congress took direct

---

2 Pennsylvania Archives, First Series, vol. x., p. 266; American Archives, Fourth Series, vol. v., p. 815; Albach's Annals of the West, Pittsburg, 1856, p. 241; McKnight's Our Western Border, 1875, pp. 389, 390.

3 American Archives, Fourth Series, vol. vi., p. 764; Fifth Series, vol. i., p. 867.

4 American Archives, Fourth Series, vol. v., p. 1654.

5 American Archives, Fourth Series, vol. vi., pp. 858-859.

control of the Indian agencies, and for the important post at Pittsburg chose George Morgan, a man of education, high family connections and considerable wealth. Morgan's home was at Princeton, N. J., his mercantile interests were in Philadelphia, and as agent of his own trading house he had traveled extensively in the Indian country, from the Allegheny to the Illinois. He arrived at Pittsburg about the first of May, 1776, and at once began to arrange for a more satisfactory treaty with the tribes. He sent agents, with pacific messages, into the Indian country, employing in this service William Wilson, Peter Long, Simon Girty and Joseph Nicholson.[6]

The mission of Wilson was the most important. He was an Indian trader and acquainted with the tribes between the Ohio river and Detroit. It was his duty to invite the Delaware, Shawnee and Wyandot chiefs to a council at Pittsburg some time in August or September. Early in June, he left Pittsburg, accompanied by Nicholson, and went on horseback to the Delaware towns on the Muskingum river. There his reception was hospitable and the chiefs of the Delawares accepted his invitation. He journeyed thence to the seats of the Shawnees on the Scioto, where he discovered many of the young warriors to be in a doubtful humor. The chief sachem, the Hardman, and the war chief, the Cornstalk, were inclined to peace and promised to attend the treaty, if possible; but they had received an invitation to take part in a great council with the British governor at Detroit, and must go there first. While Wilson was at the Shawnee towns, Morgan himself arrived there and endeavored to arrange a definite date for the treaty. The Shawnees, however, referred him to the Wyandots or Hurons, from whom the Shawnees had received permission to dwell in the Ohio country.

Before Morgan departed for Pittsburg, he gave to Wilson a large peace belt of wampum and a written message to deliver to the Wyandot chiefs. Wilson, Nicholson

---

6 Nicholson was the interpreter who accompanied Washington on his voyage down the Ohio to the Kanawha, in the fall of 1770. During his youth he had been a prisoner among the Delawares.

and the Cornstalk set out in company for the Wyandot towns on the Sandusky river, but advanced only as far as Pluggystown, on the upper Scioto. This place was inhabited by renegade Indians from various tribes, principally Iroquois. The chief, Pluggy, was a Mohawk, and his followers, called Mingoes, were horse thieves and murderers. Wilson learned that a band of these rascals had already been on a raid into Kentucky and had taken some prisoners. Pluggy's warriors formed a plot to seize Wilson and Nicholson and carry them to the British fort at Detroit. This was revealed by Cornstalk, who advised the white men to flee to the Delaware town of Coshocton. They were able to escape by night and placed themselves under the protection of old King Newcomer. That venerable sachem, believing it to be unsafe for Wilson to proceed to Sandusky, lest the Mingoes should waylay the trail, sent Killbuck, a noted war captain, to bear the American message to the Wyandot chiefs. In eleven days Killbuck returned, with word from the Wyandots that they wished to see Wilson himself, as an evidence of his good intentions, but that they could not give an answer to his invitation until they had consulted their great council beyond the lake. The chief seat of the Wyandot nation was in Canada, near Detroit, and the portion of the tribe dwelling south of Lake Erie was under the rule of a deputy chief, Dunquat, called the Half-King.

Wilson then determined to go to Sandusky and the Delaware council appointed Killbuck and two young warriors to escort him. The journey had barely begun when Killbuck fell ill and his place was taken by the celebrated White Eyes. Nicholson was no longer of the party, having gone to Pittsburg to carry a message to Morgan; but at a Delaware town on the Walhonding, Wilson was joined by John Montour, grandson of the famous Catherine Montour or Queen Esther. John was an Iroquois with an admixture of French blood, spoke English well, was master of several Indian languages and served Wilson faithfully.[7]

---

7 John Montour was the owner of Montour's Island, now called Neville's, in the Ohio river below Pittsburg, and his name is preserved by Montour Run, in Allegheny County, Pa.

Before reaching Sandusky Wilson learned that the chief there had gone to the Detroit council, and he thereupon made up his mind to venture into the immediate neighborhood of the British post, in order that he might deliver his message to the chiefs of the Wyandot nation. It was the decision of a bold man. He found the Wyandots assembled on the eastern side of the Detroit river, on the site of Windsor. By most of the chiefs he was received with apparent friendliness, and on September 2 addressed them in council, presenting his peace belt and message from Morgan, and invited them to attend at Pittsburg in 25 days from that time. The delays to which he had been subjected had forced him to postpone the date for the intended treaty. Wilson's speech was supplemented by one from White Eyes. The Wyandots, in their reply, avowed their desire for peace, but did not commit themselves on the invitation. They promised a more definite answer in two days.

On the next morning the Wyandots betrayed Wilson's presence to the British lieutenant-governor in Detroit, Col. Henry Hamilton. They returned the belt to Wilson and advised him to explain his errand to the British commander. Wilson, White Eyes and Montour were compelled to go with the Wyandot chiefs to the great council house in Detroit, where they found themselves in the presence of Colonel Hamilton and an imposing assemblage of Indian sachems. Wilson frankly announced his purpose in coming to Detroit, and, in the presence of the lieutenant-governor, again presented the peace wampum and the written message to the Wyandot chief sachem. That personage passed the articles to Colonel Hamilton.

The British commander thus addressed the Indians: "Those people from whom you receive this message are enemies and traitors to my king, and before I would take one of them by the hand I would suffer my right hand to be cut off. When the great king is pleased to make peace with his rebellious children in this big island, I will then give my assistance in making peace between them and the Indians, and not before."

Hamilton thereupon tore the speech, cut the belt into pieces and scattered the fragments about the council house. He then harangued the Wyandots on a tomahawk or war belt, but as he spoke to the interpreter in French, Wilson did not understand. Hamilton chided Montour for aiding the Americans and unsparingly denounced White Eyes, whom he ordered to leave Detroit within twenty-four hours, as he valued his life. Hamilton, notwithstanding his anger, respected Wilson's character as an ambassador and gave him safe conduct through the Indian country. The trader returned to Ft. Pitt much discouraged by the outlook and reported to Morgan that many of the Wyandots were likely to go upon the warpath in a few weeks. The Mingoes or Ohio Iroquois were already committed to hostilities.[8]

In spite of Hamilton's opposition, Indians of four tribes did attend a council with the "rebels" at Ft. Pitt in the latter part of October. The Delawares were represented by all their ruling chiefs, the Wyandots by the Half-King, the Shawnees by the great Cornstalk and a few companions, and the distant Ottawas by one sachem. Costly presents were given by the commissioners, and effusive peace speeches were made by the savages; but only the Delawares were sincere. The commissioners were persuaded that an Indian war had been averted, but they were deceived. At the conclusion of the treaty, George Morgan wrote to the president of the Congress, "The cloud which threatened to break over this part of the country appears now to be entirely dissipated."[9] While the council was being held, Indian bands were raiding the Ohio river frontier, and early in the following year all the tribes represented at the treaty, except the Delawares, were on the warpath.

---

[8] Wilson's report to George Morgan is given in the American Archives, Fifth Series, vol. ii., pp. 514-518.
[9] American Archives, Fifth Series, vol. iii., pp. 599-600.

CHAPTER IV.

CAPTURE OF ANDREW M'FARLANE.

The first depredations, in the fall of 1776, were along the eastern shore of the Ohio river, between Yellow creek and the Big Kanawha, by small parties of Mingoes from Pluggystown. It was in 1777 that the frontier war really began, with fury, on the part of the Indian tribes in general. The first outrage on the frontier of Westmoreland was the capture of Andrew McFarlane, at the outpost of Kittanning.

McFarlane, who was of Scotch descent, came from the County Tyrone, in Ireland, to Philadelphia, soon after the close of the French and Indian war, and made his way to Pittsburg. There he was employed in the Indian trade and was joined by his brother James. When the territorial dispute with Virginia became acute, in January, 1774, Andrew McFarlane was one of the additional justices of the peace appointed by Governor Penn, and he was vigorous in his efforts to uphold the Pennsylvania authority in the neighborhood of Pittsburg.[1]

In April, 1774, Captain Connolly, with his Virginia militia, interrupted the sessions of the Pennsylvania court at Hannastown and arrested the three Pennsylvania justices who lived in Pittsburg. These were Andrew McFarlane, Devereux Smith and Captain Aeneas Mackay. They were taken as prisoners to Staunton, Va., and there detained four

---

[1] Colonial Records of Pennsylvania, vol. x., under date of January 19, 1774.

weeks, until released by the order of Governor Dunmore.[2] On the evening of his arrest in Pittsburg, McFarlane managed to send a letter to Governor Penn, in which he said: "I am taken at a great inconvenience, as my business is suffering much on account of my absence, but I am willing to suffer a great deal more rather than bring a disgrace upon the commission which I bear under your honor." One result of his arrest indicates that McFarlane did not really suffer much during his captivity at Staunton. In that town the young trader formed the acquaintance of Margaret Lynn Lewis, the daughter of William Lewis, one of five brothers famous in the military history of Virginia. It must have been a case of love on sight, for Andrew McFarlane and Miss Lewis were married that summer and she went with her husband to his log home at the frontier post at the forks of the Ohio.

To escape from the exactions and persecutions of the Virginia militia officers, Andrew and his brother removed their store, in the autumn of 1774, from Fort Pitt to Kittanning, on the Allegheny, the extreme limit of white settlement toward the north. At that time probably not more than half a dozen huts existed there. Joseph Speer, another Pennsylvania trader, established a branch store at Kittanning, and the two houses soon built up a vigorous fur trade with the Indians on the tributaries of the upper Allegheny. When the Revolution came the McFarlanes were prospering.

In July, 1776, when it began to appear probable that the Iroquois were going to war, the Continental Congress ordered the raising of a Western Pennsylvania regiment, consisting of seven companies from Westmoreland and one company from Bedford, to build and garrison forts at Kittanning, Le Boeuf and Erie, to protect that region from British and Iroquois attacks by way of Lake Erie. This battalion of frontier riflemen was raised rapidly, largely out of the ranks of the Associators, and the following officers

---

2 Warner's History of Allegheny County, chapter iv. Pennsylvania Archives, First Series, vol. iv., pp. 487, 488. American Archives, Fourth Series, vol. i., p. 264.

were appointed to its command: colonel, Aeneas Mackay; lieutenant colonel, George Wilson; major, Richard Butler.[3] After its formation it went into camp at Kittanning and was there preparing for an advance up the Allegheny, to build the two other forts, when a call was received for it to march eastward, across the State of Pennsylvania, to join the hard-pressed army of General Washington on or near the Delaware.

This call raised a storm of protest on the frontier but it was not to be disobeyed, and early in January, 1777, Colonel Mackay's regiment, afterward known as the gallant Eighth Pennsylvania, set out on its long and disastrous march across the mountains.

At that time many persons, not well informed, thought the frontier was not in danger, but this was not the belief of Andrew McFarlane and his neighbors living at the exposed settlement of Kittanning. Immediately after the departure of Colonel Mackay's regiment, Magistrate McFarlane wrote to the commissioners of Westmoreland county, begging that a company of armed men be sent to Kittanning. He feared that the Iroquois would attack the little settlement. His neighbors were uneasy and he said that he remained only to keep them from running away.[4] It seems, however, that most of the other settlers at Kittanning did run away during the winter, for in February, when McFarlane was taken, the only other men at the place were two servants in charge of Joseph Speer's store.

It appears that no soldiers were at once available to occupy Kittanning and guard the stores left there by Colonel Mackay. In this emergency Samuel Moorhead, who lived at Black Lick creek, north of the Kiskiminetas, began the formation of a company of volunteer rangers for frontier protection. He chose McFarlane as his lieutenant and these two men were at work during the winter trying to embody the scattered settlers into a small company.

---

3 American Archives, Fifth Series, vol. i., pp. 1300, 1574, 1578, 1583, 1586.

4 Notes and Queries, W. H. Egle, Fourth Series, vol. i., p. 19.

CAPTURE OF ANDREW M'FARLANE.

The story of McFarlane's capture is preserved in two forms. One is gathered from letters written at the time, while the other is a tradition handed down in the Lewis family of Virginia. These two accounts illustrate the frailty of tradition as a source of historical narrative. No tale transmitted by word of mouth for two or three generations is to be relied upon unless corroborated by contemporary documents, though the tradition often forms the more interesting story. The Lewis story is now preserved in a history of Lynchburg, Va., and runs thus:

"When Margaret Lynn Lewis married Mr. McFarlane, of Pittsburg, and left the parental roof, she traveled through a wilderness infested with hostile Indians till she reached that place, where they did not consider themselves safe, constantly expecting attacks from Indians. Once, when they least apprehended danger, a warwhoop was heard, her husband taken prisoner, the tomahawk raised and she averted her eyes to avoid witnessing the fatal stroke. The river was between them, and she, with her infant and maid servant, of course, endeavored to fly, knowing the inevitable consequences of delay. After starting the servant reminded Mrs. McFarlane of her husband's money and valuable papers, but she desired the girl not to mention anything of that sort at such a moment; but, regardless of the commands of her mistress, the servant returned to the dwelling, bringing all of the money and as many of the papers as she could hold in her apron, overtaking, in a short time, her mistress, as the snow was three feet deep. On looking back she saw the house in flames, and pursuing their journey, they, with incredible fatigue, reached the house of Colonel Crawford, a distance of fourteen miles.

"Through the space of three years the brave heart of this remarkable woman was buoyed up with the firm hope and belief that she should again behold her beloved husband alive, and at length she received intelligence that he had been carried captive to Quebec, where he had encountered incredible hardships; but the chiefs had agreed that for a heavy ransom he might be restored to his friends. Of course, this ransom was paid with the greatest alacrity, his brother going on and returning with Mr. McFarlane to Staunton. In a short time the husband and wife returned to their desolated home at Pittsburg, where they literally found nothing left, the Indians having destroyed house, stock and everything pertaining to their establishment. They rebuilt their dwelling in the same spot and for many years they happily and peacefully resided there, leaving a large family, all respectably settled about Pittsburg, with the exception of two sons, who engaged in the fur trade."[4]

The contemporary account of this event is found in letters from the frontier, written to the officers of the Pennsylvania government at Philadelphia and made public in recent years.[5] The British authorities, in Canada, who were preparing to send rangers and Indians against the Western Pennsylvania border, wished to get a reliable account of the situation in the neighborhood of Fort Pitt and decided to send down a small party to take a prisoner and carry him to Canada, that he might be examined.

Two British subalterns, two Chippewas and two Iroquois were sent out by the commandment at Fort Niagara, to descend the Allegheny. At a Delaware town not far from the site of the present Franklin the white men were exhausted and stopped to rest, but the four Indians continued their journey down the west bank of the river. On February 14, 1777, they arrived opposite the little settlement of Kittanning. Standing on the shore, they shouted over, calling for a canoe. Thinking that the Indians might have come to trade or to bring important news, McFarlane decided to venture across. The instant he stepped from his boat he was seized by the savages and told that he was a prisoner.

His capture was undoubtedly seen by his wife and by two other men at the settlement, but it is not likely that a tomahawk was brandished over his head. The Indians had

---

[5] Historical Register, September, 1884; Notes and Queries, Third Series, vol. ii., p. 281; Hildreth's Pioneer History, Cincinnati, 1848, p. 114.

orders from the officer who sent them to treat their captive kindly and to return with him as quickly as possible to Niagara. To that point McFarlane was hurried, through the deep snow, and there he was subjected to the most rigid examination concerning the condition of the frontier defenses. He was then taken to Quebec. His capture caused great alarm on the border and stimulated the frontiersmen to the enrolling of the militia. Captain Moorhead hurried with his recruits to Kittanning and took charge of the houses and stores there, and all along the border preparations were made to repel the expected attacks of the savages, which came quickly with the opening of spring.

It is probable that Mrs. McFarlane did flee from Kittanning after the capture of her husband, for there was every reason to expect an Indian attack; but the place where she took refuge could not have been the house of Colonel Crawford. That gentleman lived at New Haven, on the Youghiogheny river, nearly sixty miles away, in a straight line. At the time of the capture Crawford was in Maryland, on a journey to Philadelphia. Fourteen miles would have taken the fugitives to a little settlement of two or three huts at the mouth of the Kiskiminetas river, but the nearest place of real refuge was Carnaghan's blockhouse, not less than 20 miles south of Kittanning. The Lewis tradition knows nothing of Kittanning but locates the event in the immediate vicinity of Pittsburg.

At the time of Andrew's capture his brother James was a lieutenant in the First Pennsylvania, under General Washington. It was through his efforts that Andrew was exchanged, in the fall of 1780. The released man rejoined his wife and child at Staunton, and they soon afterward returned to the vicinity of Pittsburg. Kittanning was now deserted and exposed to frequent Indian raids, and Andrew McFarlane opened a store on Chartiers creek, within the present limits of Scott township, where he lived for many years. During the later years of the Revolution he was a commissioner of purchases for the continental troops serving on the border.

His eldest son, Andrew, doubtless the infant whom Mrs. McFarlane carried in her arms when she fled from Kittanning, became one of the pioneer settlers on the Shenango, near the present New Castle, Pa., and his descendants are numerous in Lawrence county.

CHAPTER V.

GIBSON'S POWDER EXPLOIT.

When the Indian outbreak began, in the spring of 1777, the borderers found themselves in a desperate situation, because of the lack of powder. In those days, the few gunpowder factories in the colonies were all near the seaboard, and the supply for the settlers in Western Pennsylvania was carried by pack horses, in small quantities, over the mountains. It commanded a high price at Ft. Pitt, and was usually paid for with furs. Indian hostilities closed the fur trade, and made it impossible for the traders to buy powder, save on credit. This, however, was not the chief reason for the shortage. The Revolution caused a demand in the East for more powder than the factories could produce, and none could be spared for the country beyond the mountains.

To be sure, each settler kept a small stock for his own use in hunting, but in all the region around Fort Pitt there was no supply to meet the emergency of an Indian war.

The savages began to break in at many places, striking the isolated cabins, burning, murdering and pillaging. The best method of defending the scattered settlements was to organize companies of rangers, to patrol the course of the Allegheny and Ohio, and to pursue the bands of Indian marauders. Several such companies were formed, but without gunpowder they could render little service.

For a few weeks the frontier was almost helpless, but at the very verge of the crisis it was relieved by a daring exploit accomplished by a band of hardy pioneers, led by Captain George Gibson and Lieutenant William Linn. These bold adventurers descended the Ohio and Mississippi rivers to New Orleans, bought powder from the Spanish government, and successfully returned with it to Fort Pitt. This achievement has received little attention from the historians of the frontier days.

George Gibson was the son of a Lancaster tavern keeper. He had been engaged in the fur trade with his brother John at Pittsburg. In his youth he had made several voyages at sea, and he had traveled much in the Indian country. William Linn was a Marylander, who had served with Braddock as a scout and afterward settled on the Monongahela river, on the site of Fayette City. He was a farmer and a skillful hunter. He served in the Dunmore war under Major Angus McDonald and was wounded in the shoulder in a fight with the Shawnees at Wapatomika. These men were of sterling stock. A son of George Gibson became chief justice of the Supreme Court of Pennsylvania, and a grandson of William Linn became United States senator from Missouri.[1]

At the very beginning of the Revolution Gibson and Linn raised a company of young men about Pittsburg and along the Monongahela valley and entered the service of Virginia. The company marched to the Virginia seaboard, and its members so distinguished themselves for fierce valor in two conflicts with the British and tories under Dunmore that they were called "Gibson's Lambs."

They were soon sent back to the Monongahela valley, for frontier defense, and the alert and vigorous government of Virginia commissioned Gibson and Linn to undertake the hazardous journey to New Orleans.

Fifteen of Gibson's Lambs—the hardiest and the bravest—were selected to accompany the two officers. Flatboats were built at Pittsburg and the voyagers set forth on

---

[1] George Bannister Gibson, son of George Gibson, was a justice of the Supreme Court of Pennsylvania from 1816 to 1853 and chief justice for 24 years of that time. Lewis Fields Linn, grandson of Wm. Linn, was United States senator for Missouri, 1833 to 1843.

Friday, July 19, 1776. They had barely time, before their departure, to learn of the Declaration of Independence. At that time a voyage down the Ohio was extremely dangerous. The lower river was closely watched by savages. Shawnees, Miamies and Wabash Indians were already at war with the Kentucky settlements. If information of the enterprise should reach the British officers at the western posts, special endeavors would be made to intercept and destroy or capture the adventurers. The Lambs left behind them all evidences that they were soldiers. They retained their rifles, tomahawks and knives, but they were clad coarsely as boatmen or traders. Even at Pittsburg the nature of their errand was kept secret, for that frontier post was beset by tory spies. It was given out that the party was going down the river on a trading venture.

Gibson's band was both vigilant and fortunate. It passed several parties of refugees, fleeing to Fort Pitt from the Indian ravages in Kentucky. Bands of savages were all along the river, yet Gibson's barges passed unscathed. At Limestone (now Maysville, Ky.), Lieutenant Linn and Sergeant Lawrence Harrison took to the shore, and made an overland journey through Kentucky to the falls of the Ohio (now Louisville), where the barges waited for them. Both were desirous of spying out good land, and Linn afterward became a Kentucky settler. In the Kentucky woods they met John Smith, a friend, who had been hunting land, but was then on his homeward journey toward Peter's creek, on the Monongahela. Him they persuaded to accompany the expedition. The entire river voyage was made in safety, the British post at Natchez was passed in the night, and the powder hunters arrived at New Orleans in about five weeks.

Louisiana was then a Spanish province, under the governorship of Don Louis de Unzaga. Captain Gibson bore letters of commendation and credit to Oliver Pollock and other American merchants living in New Orleans. Pollock, a Philadelphian of wealth, had great influence with the Spanish authorities, and through him the negotiations for the gunpowder were conducted. Spain was at peace with Great Britain, but was ready to give secret aid to the Americans for the mere sake of weakening her traditional British enemy.

English agents in New Orleans discovered the arrival of Gibson's party, and, suspecting that their errand was to obtain munitions of war, complained to the Spanish officers that rebels against the British government were in the city. Captain Gibson was therefore arrested and lodged in a Spanish prison, where he was treated with the greatest consideration. While he was locked up Oliver Pollock secured the powder and secreted it in his warehouse. The purchase amounted to 12,000 pounds, at a cost of $1,800.

The powder was divided into two portions. Three thousand pounds of it was packed in boxes, marked falsely as merchandise of various kinds, and quietly conveyed to a sailing vessel bound by way of the gulf and ocean to Philadelphia. On the night when this ship sailed Captain Gibson "escaped" from his prison, got on board the vessel and accompanied the precious powder safely to its destination.

The greater portion of the gunpowder, 9,000 pounds, being intended for the western frontier, was turned over to the care of Lieutenant Linn. It was in half casks, each containing about sixty pounds. These casks were smuggled by night to the barges, tied up in a secluded place in the river above the city.

Lieutenant Linn hired more than a score of extra boatmen, most of them Americans, and on September 22, 1776, the little flotilla got away without discovery, and began its journey up the Mississippi. The ascent of the rivers was slow and toilsome, occupying more than seven months. At the falls of the Ohio it was necessary to unload the cargoes and to carry the heavy casks to the head of the rapids. The barges were dragged up with heavy ropes and reladen. Several times ice forced the expedition to tie up, and many hardships were endured before the return of the spring weather. On May 2, 1777, Lieutenant Linn arrived at the little settlement of Wheeling, where Fort Henry had been erected.

There he turned over his precious cargo to David Shepherd, county lieutenant of the newly erected Ohio county, Virginia.[2]

On the arrival of Gibson at Philadelphia, he communicated to the Virginia authorities the information that Linn was returning with his cargo by river. Orders were at once sent to Fort Pitt for the raising of a body of 100 militia to descend the Ohio and meet the expedition. The Ohio was considered the most dangerous part of the journey, and it was feared that Linn might be set upon and overwhelmed by savages. The officers directed to raise the relief force were so tardy in their work, that they were hardly yet ready to start when Linn's arrival at Wheeling was announced. Long as the journey was, it had been made by Linn more quickly than had been reckoned on by the frontier officers.

Lieutenant Linn's responsibility ended at Wheeling. County Lieutenant Shepherd there took charge of the powder and conveyed it, under heavy guard, to Fort Pitt, where it was given into the care of Colonel William Crawford, of the Thirteenth Virginia, and was stored in the brick-vaulted magazine of the fort. Its safe arrival was the subject of general rejoicing, and nothing was too good for Lieutenant Linn and his fearless Lambs.

The action of Virginia in this affair was liberal and patriotic. The powder had been paid for by her government and procured by her soldiers, but it was not held for her exclusive use. The receipt for it, given by Colonel Crawford, states that it was "for the use of the continent." Portions of it were distributed to the frontier rangers in the neighborhood of Fort Pitt and to the two regiments being mustered in Southwestern Pennsylvania for the continental service. It was from this stock that Colonel George Rogers Clark drew his supply, in the spring of 1778, for

---

2 The District of West Augusta, Virginia, was divided, on November 8, 1776, into Ohio, Yohogania and Monongalia counties. Yohogania county was wholly within the present limits of Pennsylvania, including Pittsburg and the lower valleys of the Monongahela and Youghiogheny rivers. The northern part of Monongalia and the eastern part of Ohio were in Pennsylvania.

his famous and successful expedition to the Illinois country.

George Gibson was promoted to the rank of lieutenant colonel in the Virginia service and William Linn was made a captain, in command of the gallant Lambs. To each officer the Virginia Legislature made a grant of money in addition to the regular pay.

Both of these men did other gallant service during the Revolution, and both were killed by Indians. Linn made a settlement about ten miles from Louisville. On March 5, 1781, while riding alone on his way to attend court at Louisville, he was surprised by a small party of Indians in the forest. Next day his mutilated body was found near the road, with his horse standing guard over it. Lieutenant Colonel Gibson was mortally wounded at St. Clair's defeat, in Northwestern Ohio, November 4, 1791, and died a few days afterward, during the retreat to the Ohio river.[3]

---

[3] Notes and Queries, vol. ii., p. 274; Third Series, vol. iii (whole No. v.), p. 421; Memoirs of John Bannister Gibson, T. P. Roberts, Pittsburg, 1890, pp. 20-21, 225.

CHAPTER VI.

THE SQUAW CAMPAIGN.

It was apparent to General Washington and other patriots that the Indian uprising which the agents of Great Britain were organizing on the frontiers was a part of the general campaign for the subjugation of the rebellious colonies. It seemed proper, under these circumstances, that the Continental Congress should take charge of the western defense, and it offered to take Fort Pitt under its care and provide a garrison at the continental expense. The offer was accepted by Virginia, and Captain Neville was directed to transfer the fort to the United States officer appointed to its command.

For this important place General Washington selected Brigadier General Edward Hand, whose brave and efficient work in the continental army led the commander to believe that he would do well in an independent command and would be an able defender of the border. Fighting British and Hessians on the seaboard and Indians in the western woods are two quite different things, as General Hand discovered in a short time.

Edward Hand was not a stranger at Fort Pitt, but during his earlier service there he had no experience in Indian warfare. He was a native of the County of Kings, Ireland, and was educated to be a physician. At the age of 23 he obtained the place of assistant surgeon in the Eighteenth Regiment of Foot, known as the Royal Irish, and in the spring of 1767 he accompanied the regiment to America.

He was stationed for a time in the Illinois country and afterward at Fort Pitt. In 1774 he resigned his commission and took up the practice of medicine at Lancaster, Pa. Soon after Lexington and Concord he interested himself in the raising of troops and was commissioned lieutenant colonel of Thompson's celebrated battalion of Pennsylvania riflemen, afterward the First Regiment of the Pennsylvania line. In March, 1776, Hand succeeded as colonel and under his command the regiment did gallant work in the battles of Long Island, Trenton and Princeton. On April 1, 1777, Hand was rewarded for his really exceptional services by promotion to the rank of brigadier general, and soon thereafter General Washington further displayed his appreciation and confidence by assigning General Hand, then 33 years old, to the Pittsburg post, to defend the western border.

It was on Sunday, June 1, 1777, that General Hand arrived at Fort Pitt and took over the property from Captain Neville. He led no force across the mountains. He was accompanied only by a few officers. His garrison consisted of but two companies of the Thirteenth Virginia, raised in and near Pittsburg and rather hard to manage. The larger part of this regiment was with Washington in New Jersey. Hand carried authority to call upon the militia officers of the frontier counties of Pennsylvania and Virginia for assistance in whatever undertaking he might plan, but he found this assistance very unreliable.

In the East, Hand had been engaged in a system of warfare where it was never difficult to find the enemy, in large bodies, ready to stand up and fight. There the Americans did most of the dodging. On the frontier the conditions were reversed. The enemy could not be found and yet seemed to be ever present. In small bands, often containing only three or four warriors, the savages entered the settlements at isolated places, struck quick but terrible blows, and then by night fled away into the forest. Where they had been was shown by dead bodies and ashes, but they left no trail that white men could discover. What could either regular troops or militia do with such a foe? To General Hand the conditions were perplexing.

Many murders had been committed before Hand's arrival, but they became more numerous in the mid-summer and autumn.[1] Colonel Hamilton, at Detroit, began, about June 1, to equip and send out war parties to attack the settlements of Kentucky, Virginia and Pennsylvania. Toward the end of July he reported to his superior at Quebec that he had sent out 15 parties, consisting of 30 white men and 289 Indians, an average of only 21 in each band.[2] These Indians were chiefly Wyandots and Miamis from Northwestern Ohio and Shawnees from Southern Ohio. At the same time parties of Senecas invaded the Pennsylvania settlements from Western New York. Beside the bodies of many of the victims of these raids were found the proclamations by Hamilton, offering protection and reward to all settlers who would make their way to any of the British posts and join the cause of the King.

General Hand had not studied the situation long when he made up his mind that there was but one way to fight the Indians; that was to invade their country and destroy their towns and provisions. The Ohio tribes were not nomadic. They had permanent villages of rude huts and grew great crops of corn, beans and pumpkins. These products were stored in large cabins or in earth silos. The hardest blow to the savages was to burn their cornfields or to destroy their garnered stores. Left without food for the winter, they were driven to the chase for subsistence, and found no time for the warpath.

Hand decided to gather a large force of militiamen, to descend the Ohio river as far as the mouth of the Big Kanawha and to march thence overland against the Shawnee towns on the Scioto. Letters were sent to the militia commanders of Westmoreland and Bedford counties, in Pennsylvania, and of all the frontier counties of Virginia,

---
1 Washington-Crawford Letters, Crawford to President of Congress, April 22, 1777; Pennsylvania Archives, First Series, viii., pp. 549, 550.
2 The Westward Movement, Winsor, Boston, 1897, pp. 111, 127.

from the Monongahela to the Kanawha, asking them to muster their men for the expedition. Hand appealed to the revolutionary governments of both states, and they directed their officers to respond to the calls. The project was even formally endorsed by the Continental Congress. In spite of all these efforts, the expedition was a failure.

Hand expected 500 men from Westmoreland and Bedford, who were to assemble at Pittsburg, and 1,500 from Western Virginia, who were to gather at two points, Fort Henry, at Wheeling, and Fort Randolph, at the mouth of the Big Kanawha.[3] His expectations were unreasonable. He did not take into account the drained and distressed condition of the border. The hardiest and most adventurous young men of this region had gone away to the East to fight the British. Most of those who remained in the scattered settlements felt that they were needed at home, to protect their own families, exposed daily to the raids of savage warriors. The Indians were penetrating to the Ligonier Valley, and even occasional outrages were perpetrated as far east as Bedford.

It seems that no men were furnished by Bedford county, and Colonel Lochry,[4] of Westmoreland, raised only 100, who marched to Fort Pitt. On October 19, 1777, General Hand left Fort Pitt and went down the river to Wheeling. There he remained about a week, waiting in vain for the assembling of a considerable body of Virginians. Only a few poorly equipped squads appeared. Hand then gave up the project and returned in disgust to Fort Pitt. The largest body of volunteers rallied at Fort Randolph, where it waited for two or three weeks without hearing a word from Hand, and then dispersed.[5]

---

[3] Ft. Pitt and Letters from the Frontier, Darlington, Pittsburg, 1892, pp. 226, 227. Chronicles of Border Warfare, Withers, pp. 151, 152. Notes and Queries, Third Series, vol. ii., Letter of Jasper Ewing to Jasper Yeates. Frontier Forts, vol. ii., p. 326.

[4] The system of county lieutenants, modeled after Virginia, was established in Pennsylvania in March, 1777, under the new state constitution. The county lieutenant was the commander of the county militia and held the rank of colonel. The Supreme Executive Council appointed Archibald Lochry county lieutenant of Westmoreland on March 21, 1777.

[5] Ft. Pitt, p. 228; Washington-Irvine Correspondence, Butterfield, Madison, Wis., 1882, p. 11. Pennsylvania Archives, First Series, vol. vi., p. 68. Frontier Forts, vol. ii., p. 244.

During October and November, while Hand was trying to form his army for the invasion of the Indian country, many raids were made in Westmoreland county. Near Palmer's Fort, in the lower end of the Ligonier Valley, 11 men were killed and scalped, and a few days later four children were killed within sight of the fort. Three men were killed and a woman was captured within a few miles of Ligonier. A band of Indians, led by a Canadian, made a fierce attack on Fort Wallace, a stockade about a mile south of Blairsville, but the white leader was killed and the assailants were repulsed. The marauders were pursued by a party of rangers, led by the celebrated Captain James Smith, who overtook the savages near Kittanning, killed five of them and triumphantly returned to the settlements with the five Indian scalps. The snow put an end to the inroads, as the Indians would not expose themselves to the certainty of being trailed in the snow.[6]

About Christmas General Hand learned that a British expedition, by lake from Detroit, had built a magazine at the mouth of the Cuyahoga river (within the present confines of Cleveland) and had stored there arms, ammunition, clothing and provisions, to be used by the Indians on the opening of spring. He saw another chance to do something for the frontier, and prepared to lead an expedition for the destruction of this magazine. He sent out calls for "brave, active lads" to assemble at Fort Pitt. He required that each man be mounted and provided with food for a short campaign. He promised to furnish ammunition and a few arms. As an incentive for enlistment, the General announced that all the plunder would be sold, and the cash proceeds divided among the members of the force. It was not until February 15 that about 500 horsemen were at Pittsburg ready for the adventure. A considerable body of them was from the Youghiogheny, under command of Colonel William Crawford. This was a formidable force and General Hand was sanguine that at last he should accomplish something.[7]

---

[6] Pennsylvania Archives, First Series, vol. v., p. 741; vol. vi., p. 68. Frontier Forts, vol. ii., p. 236, etc.

[7] Washington-Crawford Letters, pp. 66, 67.

The expedition followed the old Indian trail which descended the Ohio to the Beaver and then ascended that stream and the Mahoning toward the Cuyahoga. Snow covered the ground when Hand started, but rain soon began to fall, and continued for several days, making travel exceedingly difficult.

By the time the Mahoning was reached that stream had become excessively swollen and the crossing of its tributaries became more and more difficult. In some places the level valleys were covered with water for wide stretches. The horsemen began to grumble, and Hand was just about to give up the expedition when the foot prints of Indians were discovered on some high ground. The tracks were followed until the Americans discovered a small village of huts in a grove. This was a village of the Wolf clan of the Delawares. A sudden attack was made, but the place contained only one old man, some squaws and children. The warriors were away on a hunt. The startled savages scattered in every direction through the woods, and all escaped except three. The old man and one of the women were shot down and another woman was captured. Some of the borderers tried to kill her, but she was saved by Hand and his officers.

This affair took place about where Edenburg is, in Lawrence county. The Indian woman told her captors that ten Wolf or Muncy Indians were making salt at a lick ten miles farther up the Mahoning. Hand sent a strong detachment to take these savages, while he went into camp, under most uncomfortable circumstances, at the Indian village.

The reported Wolves turned out to be four squaws and a boy. The borderers fell upon them as fiercely as if they were Indian warriors, and killed three of the squaws and the boy. The other squaw was taken prisoner. Some defense must have been made here by the Indians, as one of Hand's men was wounded. Another man was drowned during the expedition.

It was no longer possible, on account of the weather,

THE SQUAW CAMPAIGN.

to continue the campaign, and General Hand led his dispirited and hungry men back to Fort Pitt. His trophies were two Indian women. His formidable force had slain one old man, four women and a boy. On his arrival at Fort Pitt his work was generally derided by the frontiersmen and his expedition was dubbed the Squaw Campaign.[8]

This finished Hand as the defender of the frontier. He at once wrote to General Washington a request to be relieved of his command, his request was laid before Congress, and that body, on May 2, 1778, voted his recall.[9] He could not fight Indians, but he attained distinction in other directions. He became adjutant general of the army of the United States before the close of the Revolution, was a member of Congress from Pennsylvania, and in 1798, when war was expected with France, he was made a major general in the Provisional Army. He died at Lancaster September 3, 1802.

---

8 Washington-Irvine Correspondence, p. 15. The Girtys, Butterfield, Cincinnati,/ 1890, p. 47.

9 Pennsylvania Archives, First Series, vol. vi., p. 461.

CHAPTER VII.

FLIGHT OF THE PITTSBURG TORIES.

The one event in the Revolutionary history of the border which had the most calamitous results was the flight of the tories from Fort Pitt in the spring of 1778. From the beginning of the struggle for liberty many partisans of King George were to be found on the frontier. Some of these were men who had been in the British service, most of them members of the Church of England. Others were animated by that natural reverence which many men feel for their sovereign. Many were adventurous and ambitious spirits seduced by the British promises of reward. There were some who did not believe that the Revolution would succeed, and others grew dissatisfied with the perils and the hard circumstances of frontier life in a time of war. A few were simply scoundrels, desiring turmoil and plunder. The failure of General Hand's two expeditions had much to do with the dissatisfaction with the American cause which developed on the border in the spring of 1778. During the winter the British had been in possession of Philadelphia, the American Congress had been driven to York, and Washington's army was reduced to a half-naked and half-starved remnant at Valley Forge. The cause of liberty languished, and there were many defections.

Governor Hamilton, at Detroit, sent many agents, red and white, to penetrate the border settlements, to circulate offers of pardon and reward and to organize the tories. In February and March, 1778, a daring and shrewd British spy visited Pittsburg and carried on his plotting almost under the nose of General Hand. A British flag was set up, for a short time, in the King's Orchard, which bordered the Allegheny river within gunshot of the fort, and there meetings were held by the disaffected among the soldiers of the garrison. Most of the tory gatherings in this neighborhood were at the house of Alexander McKee, at what is now called McKees Rocks. Another place of assembly was at Redstone, where a British flag flew during all of that winter.[1]

The tory leader at Pittsburg was Captain Alexander McKee, a man of education and wide influence on the border. He had been an Indian trader, and for 12 years prior to the Revolution had been the King's deputy agent for Indian affairs at Fort Pitt. For a short time he had been one of the justices of the peace for Westmoreland county. He was intimately acquainted with most of the Indian chiefs and even had an Indian family in the Shawnee nation.[2] In 1764 he received a grant of 1,400 acres of land from Colonel Bouquet, at the mouth of Chartiers creek, and he divided his time between his house in Pittsburg and his farm at McKees Rocks.

In the spring of 1776 McKee was found to be in correspondence with British officers in Canada, and he was put on his parole not to give aid or comfort to the enemies of American liberty, and not to leave the vicinity of Pittsburg without the consent of the Revolutionary Committee. In February, 1778, General Hand had reason to suspect that McKee had resumed or was continuing his correspondence with the British authorities and was organizing disaffection, and he ordered the Captain to go to York, Pa., and report himself to the Continental Congress. For a short time McKee avoided compliance with this order on the plea of sickness, but not being able to shirk obedience permanently, he decided to escape to Detroit and openly ally himself with the British cause.[3]

---
1 Deposition of John Green, Notes and Queries, Fourth Series, vol. i., p. 68.
2 Jones's Journal of Two Visits, under date of January 23, 1773.
3 American Archives, Fourth Series, vol. v., p. 815; Washington-Irvine Correspondence, p. 17.

About a year before this a young trader of the name of Matthew Elliott, who understood the Shawnee language, had been employed by the Americans to carry messages from Fort Pitt to the Shawnees and other Indian tribes to the westward, in the interest of peace. He had been made captive by hostile savages and carried to Detroit, where, after a short imprisonment, he had been released on parole. He returned to Pittsburg by way of Quebec, New York and Philadelphia, all then in British possession. He had been impressed by the show of British power in the East, in contrast with the miserable condition of the American forces. He became convinced that the Revolution would be a failure, and, on his return to Pittsburg, got into communication with McKee and others of the tory party.

Elliott is suspected of having poured into the ears of McKee a tale that he was to be waylaid and killed on his journey to York. It is certain that McKee heard such a story and believed it, and that it decided him in his plan to escape from Fort Pitt to the West.[4]

The flight of the tories took place from Alexander McKee's house during the night of Saturday, March 28, 1778. A hint of McKee's intention was given to General Hand early in the evening, and he ordered a squad of soldiers to go to McKee's house Sunday morning and remove the suspected man to the fort. The soldiers were too late.

The members of the little party which fled into the Indian land in that rough season of the year were Captain McKee, his cousin Robert Surphlit, Simon Girty, Matthew Elliott, a man of the name of Higgins, and two negro slaves belonging to McKee.[5]

Girty was a Pennsylvanian, who had been captured by the Indians when 11 years old, kept in captivity for three years by the Senecas, and afterward employed at Fort Pitt as an interpreter and messenger. Until within a few weeks

---

4 George Morgan to Henry Laurens, March 31, 1778, MS. in the Pittsburg Carnegie Library.
5 Morgan to Laurens, as in note 4; The Girtys, p. 50; Rev. A. A. Lambing, in Warner's History of Allegheny County, p. 83; Pennsylvania Archives, First Series, vol. vi., p. 445; Howe's Historical Collections of Ohio, edition of 1896, vol. i., p. 910.

FLIGHT OF THE PITTSBURG TORIES.   47

of the time of his flight he had been a faithful servitor of the American interests, and had participated earnestly in the Squaw Campaign under General Hand. In the absence of positive knowledge of the reason for his desertion, it must be presumed that he was tempted by McKee with promises of preferment in the British service.

The seven renegades made their way through the woods, which they knew well, to the chief town of the Delawares, Coshocton, where they tarried several days and endeavored to arouse that tribe to rise against the colonists. Their efforts were thwarted by White Eyes. That remarkable savage had, during the winter of 1776-7, been elected chief sachem of the Delaware nation in the place of old Newcomer, who had died in Pittsburg. White Eyes had declared his friendship for the "buckskins," as he called the Americans, and he proved his sincerity with his life.

A great debate took place in the Coshocton council, Captain Pipe, an influential chief, haranguing the savages in advocacy of war, and White Eyes pleading the cause of peace. The oratory and character of White Eyes prevailed, and the tories departed to the Shawnee towns on the Scioto. There they were welcomed. Many of the Shawnees were already on the warpath and all were eager to hear the speeches of their friend McKee. James Girty, a brother of Simon, was then with the Shawnee tribe, having been sent from Fort Pitt by the American authorities on a futile peace embassy. He had been raised among the Shawnees, was a natural savage and at once joined his brother and the other tories.[6]

Governor Hamilton heard of the escape of McKee and companions from Fort Pitt and sent Edward Hazle to the Scioto to conduct the renegades safely through the several Indian tribes to Detroit.[7] Hamilton received them cordially and gave them commissions in the British service. For 16 years McKee, Elliott and the Girtys were the mer-

---
6 Heckewelder's Narrative, p. 182; Schoolcraft's Indian Tribes, vol. vi., p. 300.
7 The Girtys, pp. 58, 59; Winning of the West, Roosevelt, vol. ii., pp. 4, 5.

ciless scourgers of the border. They were the instigators and leaders of many Indian raids and their intimate knowledge of the frontier rendered their operations especially effective. Long after the close of the Revolution they continued their deadly enmity to the American cause and were largely responsible for the general Indian war of 1790-94.

McKee and his associates left behind them a band of tories organized among the members of the Thirteenth Virginia, of which a detachment was stationed in Fort Pitt. These rascals had formed a plot to blow up the fort and escape in boats by night. In some way this scheme was frustrated at the last moment, probably by the confession of one of the conspirators, and the explosion was prevented. Sergeant Alexander Ballantine and about a score of the traitors were able to get away in one of the large boats belonging to the post, and in the night of April 20 fled down the Ohio river. On the following day they were pursued by a large party of their comrades and were overtaken near the mouth of the Muskingum. Eight of the runaways escaped to shore and were lost in the trackless woods, some were killed in conflict on the spot and others were returned as prisoners to Fort Pitt. They were tried by a court-martial, of which Colonel William Crawford was president.

The leaders were found to be Sergeant Ballantine, William Bentley and Eliezer Davis. Two of these were shot and the other was hanged. Two other men were publicly whipped on the fort parade ground, each receiving 100 lashes on the bare back.[8]

The punishment of these men was almost the last act performed by General Hand before his departure for the East. For a time it put an end to the machinations of the tories at Pittsburg, but it marked the beginning of the most cruel and disastrous warfare since the uprising of the tribes under Pontiac in 1763.

---

[8] Washington-Irvine Correspondence, p. 18; The Girtys, p. 53; Pennsylvania Archives, Second Series, vol. iii., p. 189.

CHAPTER VIII.

THE TORIES OF SINKING VALLEY.

One of the melancholy tragedies of the revolutionary frontier is connected with the effort of a band of tories to escape from Bedford county and join the British and Indians on the Allegheny river. While the tory plotting, which led to the flight of McKee, Girty and associates, was going on at Fort Pitt, during the winter of 1777-78, British agents were busy at many places on the western border seeking to corrupt the frontier settlers. During that winter these agents, from Niagara and Detroit, visited the lonely settlements of Bedford and Westmoreland counties, insinuating sentiments of discontent into the minds of the border farmers, assuring them that the American cause was sure to fail, and making glittering promises of reward for those who should join the cause of the King.

One of these agents, who spent the winter months in the valleys of the Alleghany Mountains, in what is now Blair county, but was then a part of Bedford, was successful in deluding a considerable band of ignorant frontiersmen by the most despicable methods.

The villain did not confine himself to the promises authorized by the British authorities, as endorsed by Governor Hamilton, of Detroit. These promises were that any man who deserted the American cause and joined the British should have 200 acres of land, on the conclusion of peace, and that any officer of the American forces should receive a corresponding commission under the King. The rascal who worked among the mountaineers held out to them a vision of wholesale plunder and carnage on the property and lives of their patriot neighbors. His appeals were made only to the vicious. He told them that if they would organize and join a force of British and Indians, coming down the Allegheny valley in the spring, they would be permitted to participate in a general onslaught on the settlements, and would receive their share of the pillage. In addition to this, they should receive grants for the lands of their rebel neighbors, to the extent of 300 acres each, wherever they should select.[1]

One of the men who entered into this desperate plot afterward confessed that it was the design to slaughter the peaceable inhabitants without mercy, men, women and children, and to sieze their property and lands. Such a scheme could be taken up only by men of the lowest character and the most cruel instincts, but such men were not wanting on the border, either at that time or in later years, when the frontier had been pressed hundreds of miles farther to the westward.

In the northern part of Blair county is a deep valley amid the mountains, called Sinking Spring valley. It is still a wild and romantic country, but 120 years ago was a singularly desolate and lonely spot, almost unknown, except to those few persons who lived in the immediate neighborhood. It was a fitting place for the meeting of such conspirators as had been enlisted in this cruel tory plot. In that isolated valley the tory band held its gatherings in February and March, 1778. Many of the plotters were from the frontier settlement of Frankstown, near what is now Hollidaysburg. The leader of the enterprise was John Weston, a bold and lawless man, half farmer and half hunter, who lived with his wife and brother Richard in one of the secluded mountain cabins.

The British agent, having fully enlisted Weston in the murderous undertaking, returned up the Allegheny, prom-

---

1 See the confession of Richard Weston, Pennsylvania Archives, First Series, vol. vi., p. 542.

THE TORIES OF SINKING VALLEY. 51

ising to come to Kittanning about the middle of April with 300 Indians and white men, there to meet his mountain friends, and with them swoop down on Fort Pitt, Frankstown and the other settlements, and make all of his partisans weary with the burden of their rich plunder.

Weston carried on the propaganda, and early in April had enlisted some 30 of his neighbors in the adventure. All were ignorant men, Irish, German and Scotch settlers, although it appears that only one Scotch family was involved.

Alarming intelligence of the tory plans leaked out and reached the settlement of Standing Stone, now Huntingdon. It was reported that a thousand Indians and tories were about to fall on the frontier, and the greatest alarm was felt. Although a stockade fort had been erected at the Standing Stone, it had a garrison of not more than a score of militiamen, and the borderers did not feel that it would afford protection. There was a general flight of the terrified people from the upper valley of the Juniata toward Carlisle and York, and by the middle of April that region of country was depopulated except by a party of bold men who still held the little fort, determined to stand until the last.

The band of schemers meeting in the Sinking Spring valley was joined, about the first of April, by a man of the name of McKee, who came from Carlisle. There he had been in communication with a British officer confined at Carlisle with other prisoners of war. The officer gave to McKee a letter addressed to all British officers, vouching for the loyalty of McKee and his associates. It was to be used in securing protection and a welcome for the Sinking Spring plotters when they should meet with the force of British and Indians on their flight to the Allegheny.

At the appointed time word reached the valley that a large force of Indians had gathered at Kittanning, where they had occupied the rude fort deserted by the Americans in the preceding year. Weston and his associates felt that their time had come, and that their enterprise was assured of success. The last meeting of the tories was held in the forest, at the loneliest spot in the glen. There 31 men took the oath of fidelity to King George, and pledged themselves to adhere to Weston.

In the morning they set out on their march over the mountains. They crossed the main range at Kittanning Point and struck the old Indian trail leading toward Kittanning. On the afternoon of the second day they came within a few miles of their destination, when they encountered a band of Iroquois Indians, numbering about 100. The savages burst suddenly out of a thicket, clad in war paint and feathers.

John Weston, who was in advance of his party, ran forward, waving his hand and crying out, "Friends! Friends!" The Indians were not in the conspiracy. They were out on a plundering raid, on their own account, and regarded Weston and his men, all armed, as a hostile array.

The Indian war captain fired at Weston. The aim was quick but accurate, and the tory leader fell dead. His followers halted in dread astonishment. Another of the savages sprang forward, and, before the ignorant borderers could recover from their surprise or comprehend what was being done, tore the scalp from Weston's head. The savage uttered the scalp halloo and darted back into the thicket.

McKee, holding aloft in one hand the letter from the British officer at Carlisle, and in the other hand waving a white handkerchief, called out to the Indians, "Brothers! Brothers!" The savages did not respond. Almost as suddenly as they had appeared they vanished into the undergrowth, leaving the bewildered mountaineers alone with their dead and mutilated leader. Weston was buried where he had fallen, and his resting place was unmarked. It was a just end for one who had entertained such sanguinary projects.

The thirty other tories, left leaderless, in a wilderness, whence hostile savages sprang apparently from the very earth, were completely dazed and disorganized. They feared to go forward; many of them feared to return to their homes. They retired to a sheltered place and held a consultation. Some declared their intention to return to Bedford county, but those who were best able to appreciate the nature of their offense apprehended arrest and announced that they would seek safety elsewhere.[2]

Hard was the fate of this company. Some of them wandered in the forests and perished from hunger. Others made their way southward, and reached British posts in the southern colonies after great suffering. Five of them, returning to their homes, were seized by the aroused frontiersmen, and conducted to the log jail in Bedford. Richard Weston, brother of the dead leader, was caught in Sinking Spring valley by a party of Americans going to work the lead mines there, and was sent under guard to Carlisle. He confessed the whole plot, but claimed that he had been misled by his older brother. He escaped from imprisonment before he could be brought to trial.[3]

A special court, of which General John Armstrong, of Carlisle, was president, was appointed by the Supreme Executive Council to try the prisoners at Bedford. It held two sessions in the fall of 1778 and the spring of 1779, but did not convict any of the defendants of high treason. The leaders of the conspiracy were either dead or out of the country, and the few men brought before the court were but ignorant and deluded yeomen, who were sufficiently punished by their imprisonment and the contempt of their neighbors.[4]

Those who had fled away were attainted of treason, and their estates were declared forfeited. It appears that a few of them returned to Pennsylvania, after the war was over, and procured the removal of the attainder and the restoration of their land.

[2] Day's Historical Collections of Pennsylvania, p 372; Pennsylvania Archives, First Series, vol. vi., pp. 436, 438, 446, 467, 469, 542; Lytle's History of Huntingdon County, Lancaster, 1876, pp. 80, 283; Jones's History of the Juniata Valley, Philadelphia, 1856, pp. 250-257.
[3] His escape is shown by the fact that he was attainted of treason with all those who fled to the southern states; see Pennsylvania Archives, First Series, vol. x., p. 259.
[4] The court did not report any treason convictions to the Supreme Executive Council, but did report one conviction for murder, Colonial Records, vol. xi., p. 581. See, also, on this court, Colonial Records, vol. x., p. 556; Pennsylvania Archives, First Series, vol. vi., pp. 569, 750, 769; vol. vii., p. 297.

CHAPTER IX.

FATAL VOYAGE OF DAVID RODGERS.

An attempt was made, in 1778, to repeat the feat of Gibson and Linn, in bringing powder from New Orleans by river. The store of ammunition conveyed to Fort Pitt by Lieutenant Linn, in the spring of 1777, had been almost exhausted. A large part of it had been taken to Kentucky, Vincennes and Kaskaskia by George Rogers Clark, and much of it had been used for the defense of the immediate frontier.

The second undertaking was, like the first, ordered and directed by the government of Virginia. In this instance the powder was bought in advance, by correspondence with Oliver Pollock, and was transported by the Spaniards from New Orleans to the little post of St. Louis, where the Spaniards had established their authority in 1768. It seems that the removal of the powder to St. Louis was not understood in Virginia, and the expedition which went after it lost much time in going down the Mississippi to find it.

To organize and command the second expedition, Governor Patrick Henry chose Captain David Rodgers, of Redstone. This gentleman was a native of Old Virginia, and had been engaged with distinction in the frontier conflicts of that colony. He settled on a farm near the present site of Brownsville, Pa., about 1773, and in March, 1775, was appointed a Virginia justice of the peace for the district of West Augusta, which included Southwestern Pennsylvania. He sat in court at Pittsburg and at Andrew Heath's house, near Monongahela. When the news of Lexington and Concord reached the frontier, in May, 1775, David Rodgers took part in the patriotic meeting held at Pittsburg and was elected a member of the revolutionary committee of West Augusta. He entered the Virginia service and became a captain. Before proceeding on his Louisiana adventure he sent his wife and children to Oldtown, Md., for safety. They never saw him again.

When he received his orders from Governor Henry, in the spring of 1778, to bring the powder from New Orleans, he raised a special company of men in what was then known as the Redstone settlement. The band numbered about 40. Most of its members were hardy young farmers, but not many of them were experienced in military service. Isaac Collie was commissioned lieutenant, Patrick McElroy ensign, and Robert Benham commissary.

Two large flatboats, partially covered, were built at Pittsburg. These were operated by long sweeps and a steering pole. One of them was taken up the Monongahela to Redstone and there received a stock of provisions and the men who were to make the expedition. Among those who embarked was Basil Brown, younger brother of Thomas Brown. These brothers were the sons of Thomas Brown, and were the founders of Brownsville.

The expedition of Captain Rodgers left Fort Pitt in June, 1778. For some days it was accompanied by two family boats, carrying settlers to Kentucky. The voyage down the Mississippi, as far as the mouth of the Arkansas river, passed without special incident. Rodgers entered the Arkansas and ascended it a few miles to a small Spanish fort. There he learned that the powder had been sent up the Mississippi to St. Louis.

Having had no communication with the Spanish commander at St. Louis, Captain Rodgers considered it necessary to go to New Orleans, and there procure, from the governor, an order on the St. Louis officer for the powder. He left his boats and most of his men at the post on the

Arkansas, embarked with six companions in a large canoe, and floated down to the Spanish capital of Louisiana. There he obtained the paper which he desired, and set out on his return.

Not wishing to take a second risk, especially on an up-stream, by passing the British fort at Natchez, Rodgers and his comrades returned overland from New Orleans to the Arkansas. This was a toilsome and dangerous tramp through the swamps and forests along the western shore of the great river. Doubtless the little party had a guide, for, after many wearisome days, it came safely to the place where the flatboats lay in the Arkansas. The voyage thence to St. Louis was made successfully, and the powder was procured. At that time St. Louis had a population of about 800 persons, mostly French refugees from the Illinois. The Spanish garrison, of 100 soldiers, was under the command of Don Francisco de Leyba. The sale by the Spaniards of this powder to the Americans was a violation of international law, but its actual delivery to Rodgers probably did not take place until after Spain had declared war against Great Britain in May, 1779.[1]

The slow and laborious voyage up the Ohio, with the heavily laden flatboats, was made during the summer and autumn, and all went well until the expedition reached the Licking river, opposite the site of Cincinnati. That region then was unbroken wilderness, nearly the whole course of the Ohio being bordered by great forests, with dense undergrowth.

At the mouth of the Licking, the great Indian warpath from the Maumee and the valleys of the two Miamis, struck the Ohio valley, on the way to Kentucky and the land of the Cherokees. As Indian bands were frequently crossing there, it was a point of danger for boats passing up and down the Ohio.

On an October afternoon, as the craft of Rodgers approached the mouth of the Licking, keeping rather close to the Kentucky shore, a few Indian warriors, in three or

---

[1] Annals of the West, pp. 312, 313.

four canoes, were discovered crossing the Ohio to the southern shore, nearly a mile up stream. The savages gave no sign that they had seen the Americans, and Rodgers believed that his boats, close to the heavy foliage of the bank, had not been observed. He had no doubt that the Indians were on their way to attack some Kentucky settlement. He decided, therefore, to land his party and attempt to surprise and destroy the savages in the woods.

The flatboats were guided into the mouth of the Licking and pulled up on a sandy beach at the southeastern point between the two rivers. The scene of the ensuing conflict is now occupied by the town of Newport, Ky.

Being confident of overcoming easily the small party of savages, the Americans advanced into the woods with some eagerness. They had not penetrated far when they rushed into an ambush. They had been cleverly entrapped. The few warriors crossing the river in the canoes were but decoys. A strong force of savages, led by Simon Girty and Matthew Elliott, lay hidden in the dense forest. They outnumbered the white men two to one. On every side they sprang up amid the underbrush, shrieking their terrifying warwhoops, pouring a deadly fire into the astonished borderers.

Many of the Americans fell at the first discharge, and panic seized the remainder. They were almost instantly overwhelmed and scattered. With tomahawk and knife, the savages rushed in upon them, and the only hope of escape for any one was by rapid flight through the forest. Many of the frontiersmen were slain and scalped on the spot, and others were overtaken and killed in the woods as they ran. It was only because of the denseness of the undergrowth and the quick approach of night that any escaped. Of the company of 40 men, only 13 got away with their lives. Some of these were sorely wounded and endured great agony in the wilderness. Those who were unscathed made their way to the little settlements in the interior of Kentucky.

Captain Rodgers received a bullet wound in the abdomen, but managed by the help of John Knotts to get away from the scene of conflict and hide in a dark ravine. Fortunately for the hunted Americans, nightfall soon put an end to the pursuit. The scattered savages called to one another with wierd cries, soon assembled, and after plundering the flatboats on the Licking beach, went entirely away. Their trophies were enough to satisfy them, and they probably crossed to the north side of the Ohio that night.

All through the darkness Captain Rodgers lay in great torment. Knotts could do nothing for him save to make his resting place soft and to bring water from a neighboring brook. In the morning the wounded man was delirious and evidently near death. Knotts felt it to be his duty to save himself, if he could. He screened the form of the dying Captain with bushes and set out through the wilderness. After great hardship he reached his home on the Monongahela. Afterward search was made for the body of Captain Rodgers, but it could not be found. It had probably been torn to pieces by wolves.

Robert Benham, the commissary of the expedition, was wounded through both legs, but was able to conceal himself in the top of a fallen tree. He had clung to his rifle, but for a long time feared to fire it or to make other alarm, lest the Indians might still be in the neighborhood. It was not until the afternoon of the second day after the battle that hunger persuaded him to shoot a raccoon which ventured within his range. The sound of his gun had scarcely died away when he heard the call of a human voice. He suspected that it was the shout of a savage, and hurriedly reloaded his rifle; but footsteps were soon heard in the thicket, and a haggard and ragged white man, covered with blood, pushed his way through. It was Basil Brown. He was wounded in the right arm and the left shoulder, so that both hands hung helpless at his sides. He, like Benham, had been in hiding until he heard the sound of the rifle shot.

Here, in the wilderness woods, were two wounded

Americans, having between them only one pair of good arms and one pair of good legs! It was a singular situation, and it was a queer partnership of mutual aid which they formed for their preservation. Benham pointed out the dead raccoon. Brown kicked it to the place where Benham reclined. The latter built a fire, dressed and cooked the animal and fed his companion as well as himself.

To procure water, Benham placed a folded hat between Brown's teeth and Brown then waded into the Licking river, dipped the hat into the water and carried it full to his thirsty comrade. Thus these two men in distress supplemented the actions of one another for many days. Brown made wide circuits in the woods, shouting and kicking the underbrush, driving rabbits, squirrels and wild turkeys within the range of Benham's accurate rifle. When the game had been brought down, Brown kicked it to the fire and Benham did the rest.

Every day Brown spent much of his time on the bank of the Ohio, watching for a passing boat. It was not until 19 days after the disaster that a flatboat descending the river was attracted by Brown's cries. The wounded men were rescued and taken to the new settlement at the falls of the Ohio (Louisville). After their wounds were healed they returned to their homes at Redstone, and both lived for many years afterward. Basil Brown died about 1835, at the age of 75. He never married, but lived at Brownsville with his crippled sister, Sally. Robert Benham, when the war was over, bought and settled on the land where Rodgers met his disaster and death, and was one of the pioneers of Newport.[2]

---

2 Annals of the West, p. 306; Affidavit of Basil Brown, in Notes and Queries, Third Series, vol. iii., p. 423; Howe's Hist. Coll. of Ohio, vol. ii., p. 741; Winning of the West, Roosevelt, vol. ii., p. 136; The Girtys, p. 110.

CHAPTER X.

THE EIGHTH PENNSYLVANIA.

The activities of the tories and the excessive malignity of the Indian attacks on the frontier, in the spring of 1778, alarmed the Continental Congress. It recommended to Washington that more vigorous measures be taken to defend the western border. The Commander-in-Chief, hard pressed as he was in the East, responded promptly to the appeal. Congress voted the recall of General Hand on May 2, and on the same day Washington appointed Brigadier General Lachlan McIntosh to succeed in the command at Fort Pitt.[1] Three weeks later the Eighth Pennsylvania and the Thirteenth Virginia were detached from the army at Valley Forge—an army already too small—and ordered to march to the Ohio river.[2]

McIntosh was a Scotch Highlander, 53 years old. He was born near Inverness, the son of the head of the Borlam branch of the Clan McIntosh. When the boy was 11 years old, his father and mother, with other Highlanders, left their native land and joined General Oglethorpe's new colony of Georgia. The McIntosh settled a plantation near the mouth of the Altamaha river, in what is now McIntosh county. A few years later the father was captured by the Spaniards, and died in a prison at St. Augustine.

Lachlan McIntosh owed most of his education to his excellent mother. At 17 he entered a mercantile house in

---
1 Pennsylvania Archives, First Series, vol. vi., pp. 460, 461, 467, 528.
2 Pennsylvania Archives, First Series, vol. vi., pp. 556, 564.

Charleston, but an indoor life was not to his liking. As soon as he was a man, he returned to the plantation, learned the trade of surveyor, and took an active interest in the militia. He married a Highland woman, and became a leader in his part of the colony.

While many of the Scots of Georgia adhered to the cause of King and Parliament, McIntosh was an enthusiastic American, and at the outburst of the Revolution became a colonel in the colonial service. In 1776 he was made a brigadier general. In 1777 he became involved in a quarrel with Button Gwinnett, one of the signers of the Declaration. Gwinnett challenged McIntosh to a duel, and the challenger was mortally wounded. McIntosh was tried for murder and acquitted, but the resulting feud rendered life in Georgia unpleasant and unprofitable. He asked for a transfer, and early in 1778 was ordered to join Washington at Valley Forge. The Georgia Scotchman at once made a good impression on the great Commander-in-Chief. In writing to Congress of his appointment of McIntosh to the western command, Washington said: "I part with this gentleman with much reluctance, as I esteem him an officer of great worth and merit, and as I know his services here are and will be materially wanted. His firm disposition and equal justice, his assiduity and good understanding, added to his being a stranger to all parties in that quarter, point him out as a proper person."[3] Such was the man who went, with high expectations, to succeed Hand as the defender of the Pennsylvania frontier.

It was at the request of the Board of War that Washington ordered two regiments of regulars to Fort Pitt, and the regiments chosen were the two that had been raised about the headwaters of the Ohio. In marching to what was then the far West, the men of these commands were simply marching home. Because they were frontiersmen, already acquainted with Indian warfare, Washington be-

---

[3] Washington's Letters to the American Congress, New York, 1796, vol. ii., p. 224.

lieved that they would be the most effective defenders of the border.[4]

The Eighth Pennsylvania was one of the notable organizations of the Revolution, and well deserves to be remembered by succeeding generations, especially in Western Pennsylvania, where live many of the descendants of its brave officers and privates. Seven of its companies were raised in Westmoreland, and the eighth in Bedford county. The names of most of its officers are still familiar names in Westmoreland, Allegheny, Washington and Fayette. The original staff officers, commissioned by Congress in the summer of 1776, were: Colonel, Aeneas Mackay, of Pittsburg; Lieutenant Colonel, George Wilson, of George's creek, Fayette county; Major, Richard Butler, Indian agent at Pittsburg; Quartermaster, Ephraim Douglass, a Pittsburg trader; Commissary, Ephraim Blaine, great-grandfather of James G. Blaine; Adjutant, Michael Huffnagle, of Hannastown; Chaplain, David McClure; Paymaster, John Boyd, of Pittsburg.[5]

With the exceptions of Ephraim Blaine and David McClure, the officers and men were frontiersmen. Blaine was an Ulsterman, of the Cumberland Valley, a merchant and landed proprietor, a man of great energy, who became afterward commissary general of the revolutionary army. Rev. David McClure was a native of Rhode Island, of Ulster parentage, who went as a missionary to the Delaware Indians in the Tuscarawas valley in 1772. Being rejected by the savages, he remained in Westmoreland county as an itinerant preacher until June, 1773, when he returned to New England, and there spent the remainder of his life. He never joined the regiment to which he was appointed chaplain.[6]

The captains were Van Swearingen, Moses Carson, Samuel Miller, James Piggott, Wendel Ourry, David Kill-

---

[4] Washington-Crawford Letters, Washington to the Board of War, May 23, 1778.

[5] American Archives, Fifth Series, vol. i., pp. 1574, 1578, 1583, 1586; vol. ii., pp. 1333, 1338, 1405.

[6] See Diary of David McClure, New York, 1899.

gore, Eliezer Myers and Andrew Mann. Of these, Carson was the only one who proved false to his country.[7]

The nucleus of the regiment was the company of riflemen formed by Van Swearingen, in May, 1776, for defense against the Indians. Swearingen was one of the noted characters of the border. With his father and brothers, he moved from Virginia and became a pioneer of the upper Monongahela valley. He was of great stature and fearless spirit. By the time of the Revolution he had acquired on the frontier the name of "Indian Van." One of his brothers was captured by the Indians, and became a chief of the Shawnee nation.

Swearingen's company was stationed at Kittanning for two months and then joined the new continental battalion, ordered by Congress on July 11, 1776. The purpose of the organization of this battalion or regiment was to garrison the western posts and protect the frontier. It was an easy matter to recruit the borderers for the defense of their own homes, and the very best men of Westmoreland joined the organization. Between August 9 and December 16, 1776, 630 men were enlisted.

Mackay's battalion, as it was formed, went into camp at Kittanning, where the men built their own rude cabins for the winter. They had settled down for the cold season, sending out scouting parties up and down the river, when, on December 4, the regiment was surprised by the receipt of an order from the Continental Congress to march to New Jersey and join the army of General Washington. At that time the Commander-in-Chief was being driven, by the British, across New Jersey to the Delaware river, Philadelphia was in danger, the Revolution seemed to be at its lowest ebb, great alarm prevailed in the East, and the call for aid went out to all parts of the colonies. The Eighth Pennsylvania, encamped on the Allegheny river, was the most distant command summoned to the support of the patriot cause.

---

7 American Archives, Fifth Series, vol. ii., p. 1340.

The order caused much discontent in Mackay's battalion, for officers and men felt it a hardship to be called away from the duty for which they had enlisted, leaving their families unprotected in the face of an impending Indian warfare. The regiment, moreover, was badly provided for a mid-winter march over the mountain ranges. It was without uniforms or tents, and was scantily furnished with blankets and cooking utensils. Yet there was little hesitation. The scouting parties were called in, pack horses were collected, and the command began its desperate journey on January 6, 1777, at the very worst period of the Pennsylvania winter.[8]

This was a trying march across the state, along bad roads, amid deep snows, by mountain passes, through desolate forests, without tents or sufficient food or clothing. The whole distance exceeded 300 miles, of which more than 100 was through a region of rough mountains and their intervening valleys. Encampments were made in the most sheltered places, amid heavy timber, and great fires were kept going all night, that the men might not perish from the cold. Hunting parties procured some meat, but for most of the journey the only food consisted of cakes and bread. Arnold's winter toil through the Maine woods into Canada was the only march of the Revolution that exceeded this in severity.

It is not surprising that some of the men deserted and returned to their homes. Toward the end of February the regiment reached Quibbletown, near Philadelphia, and went into camp in miserable quarters. One-third of the men were ill, and within two weeks there were 50 deaths. Among those who died as the result of their terrible privations were Colonel Mackay and Lieutenant Colonel Wilson.[9]

---

8 Pennsylvania Archives, First Series, vol. v., p. 93. For the early history of the regiment, its winter march and service in the east, see Pennsylvania Archives, Second Series, vol. x., pp. 641-648.

9 Pennsylvania Archives, First Series, vol. v., p. 283. Many writers have identified Colonel Aeneas Mackay with the Captain James Mackay, of South Carolina, who assisted Washington in the defense of Ft. Necessity in 1754. This is a mistake. Aeneas Mackay came to America about 1767 as a commissary with the Royal Irish regiment (Eighteenth Foot). For a sketch of the life of Lieutenant Colonel George Wilson, see Veech's Monongahela of Old.

THE EIGHTH PENNSYLVANIA. 65

While this perilous march was making, Washington had won the victories of Trenton and Princeton, had relieved Pennsylvania from the danger of immediate invasion, and had taken post, with his little army, north of the Raritan river, in New Jersey. To that place, after a short rest, the Eighth proceeded, and there it received new officers. Daniel Brodhead became colonel; Richard Butler was promoted to be lieutenant colonel, and Stephen Bayard, a son-in-law of Aeneas Mackay, was made major. The regiment was placed in the second brigade of General Anthony Wayne's Pennsylvania division.

In June Washington formed Morgan's famous rifle corps, of the best sharp-shooters to be found in the whole army. There is a general impression that this corps of 500 dead-shots was made up of Virginians, but this is an error. Virginia contributed only 163 men. More were chosen from the Eighth Pennsylvania than from any other command. It furnished 139, including Lieutenant Colonel Butler and Captain Swearingen. The First Pennsylvania furnished 54 men, from that part of the regiment recruited on the upper Susquehanna, among the number being the celebrated Lieutenant Samuel Brady.[10] This corps was sent to the northern army under General Gates. It did the most effective fighting at Stillwater and Saratoga, and participated in the triumph when Burgoyne surrendered.

Late in the fall Morgan rejoined Washington near Philadelphia. The men of the Eighth Pennsylvania returned to their regiment, and Lieutenant Brady was transferred to that organization. Thus he obtained the opportunity which gave him lasting fame on the western border. The portion of the regiment which had remained with Washington's army had been engaged, under Wayne, in the defeats of Brandywine, Paoli and Germantown, and the reunited command passed the winter of 1777-78 in the distressful encampment of Valley Forge.

Daniel Brodhead, who led the Eighth Pennsylvania back to the West and subsequently acted an important part

---

10 Pennsylvania Archives, Second Series, vol. x., pp. 311-313, 315, 643.

in the history of the frontier, was the son of a pioneer tavern-keeper living near the Delaware Water Gap. He had early experience in Indian war, learned surveying, settled in Reading, and took a prominent part in the agitation against the oppressions of the British Parliament. He was a member of the Pennsylvania convention in 1775, raised soldiers for the revolutionary army, and in 1776 became a lieutenant colonel in the Pennsylvania service. He acquitted himself gallantly in the battle of Long Island, August 27, 1776, and won promotion. He was a man of energy and persistence, bold in planning, fearless in executing, keen to assert his authority, well set in his opinions and of hasty temper.

The other regiment ordered to Fort Pitt, the Thirteenth Virginia, had been raised by Colonel William Crawford in the territory now included in the counties of Fayette, Washington and Greene. Its formation in 1777 had been somewhat slow, and before it was completed about 200 of the men were ordered to the East. The remainder of the command, about 100 men, when enlisted, was detained at Fort Pitt, and was still there, under Colonel William Russell, when the eastern detachment, with Washington's army, was ordered to return to the West.

Lieutenant Colonel John Gibson was promoted to the rank of colonel, went west with the main part of the regiment, and took command of the reunited force under McIntosh. Colonel Russell was called to the East.[11]

---

[11] Washington's Letters to the American Congress, vol. ii., pp. 229, 232.

CHAPTER XI.

BACK TO THE HARRIED FRONTIER.

In both of its marches across the state of Pennsylvania, the Eighth regiment was unfortunate. The first, from Kittanning to Philadelphia, was made in the dead of winter; the second, from Valley Forge to Fort Pitt, was in the heat of midsummer, and included a long diversion up the valley of the Susquehanna.

General McIntosh, with the detachment of the Thirteenth Virginia, left camp toward the end of May and marched to Lancaster, where the fugitive Congress was in session. The Eighth Pennsylvania, under Colonel Brodhead, did not march from Valley Forge until the middle of June, and then proceeded by way of Lancaster to Carlisle. Before their departure into the borderland the men of the Westmoreland regiment received uniforms. The officers were outfitted with the traditional blue of the continental line, but the men were clad in hunting shirts, with broad-brimmed hats looped up, and long leggings. When organized in the West, the men carried long rifles, but these were replaced, on the advice of General Wayne, by muskets and bayonets, with the exception of a small detachment of sharp-shooters, who retained their rifles for scouting and skirmishing work.

While the Thirteenth Virginia pushed onward, over the mountain road toward the Ohio, General McIntosh waited at Carlisle until the Eighth regiment arrived there early in July. The most alarming news had been received from the upper branches of the Susquehanna. In May the Iroquois came down on the scattered settlements of the West Branch and in two weeks killed and captured more than 30 persons. This caused what was known as the Big Runaway, when nearly all the settlers on the West Branch, from Bald Eagle creek down to the junction with the North Branch, fled by boats, on horses and afoot to Sunbury, Carlisle, York and Lancaster. Great was the suffering of the thousands of fugitives.[1] General McIntosh reached the Susquehanna to find himself surrounded and beset by the fleeing settlers and their families, crying for protection and relief. He determined to send some of his troops up the Susquehanna to stop the Indian incursions, but before the Eighth arrived at Carlisle the news of a greater calamity was received.

On the 3d of July, 1778, took place the "massacre" of Wyoming, most notably but untruthfully commemorated by Thomas Campbell in his poem, "Gertrude of Wyoming." Four hundred British and tories and 700 Iroquois Indians, from Central New York, burst into the beautiful valley on the North Branch of the Susquehanna with gun, tomahawk, scalping knife and torch, and in a few days swept it clean of its inhabitants and habitations.

At once Colonel Brodhead was ordered to march up the Susquehanna, drive out the enemy and encourage the settlers to return to their plantations. The baggage and pack horses were left at Carlisle, and on July 12, the regiment marched in light order, about 340 strong.[2] Several small detachments had already preceded the regiment on the road toward Fort Pitt, to prepare provisions for the men and forage for the horses at points along the route. The command hurried to Sunbury, where Fort Augusta was held by 100 bold volunteers. From that place Colonel Brodhead sent details up both branches of the great river.

The British and Indians had retired from the Wyoming

---

1 Pennsylvania Archives, First Series, vol. vi., pp. 499, 615, 631; Day's Hist. Coll. of Pa., p. 451.
2 Pennsylvania Archives, First Series, vol. vi., p. 635.

BACK TO THE HARRIED FRONTIER. 69

valley and the commander found that it was too late to assist the inhabitants there against their enemy. The ruin had been wrought, and all the settlers had either been killed, carried away captives or driven across the mountains toward the Delaware river.

On the West Branch the situation was not quite so bad, for there the harvests had not been destroyed, and many cabins were yet standing. It became Brodhead's duty to clear the region of bands of prowling savages, guard the trails and place detachments at the principal centers of settlement to encourage the farmers to return and do their harvesting.

Major Butler was sent up the North Branch to Nescopec, with two companies; Captain John Finley, who had succeeded Moses Carson when that individual deserted, was detailed with his company into Penn's valley, west of the Susquehanna, and with the remainder of the command Brodhead advanced up the West Branch to Muncy, to cover the harvesters in that rich agricultural region. On July 24 Brodhead wrote from Muncy: "Great numbers of the inhabitants returned upon my approach, and are now collected in large bodies, reaping their harvests."[3]

The Nescopec and Muncy detachments had few opportunities to fire their muskets at skulking Indians, but the men of Captain Finley's company, sent into Penn's valley, had the only serious encounter. They were posted at the settlement of Colonel James Potter, the pioneer of that region, who had built a stockade around his house, about nine miles southeast of the present town of Bellefonte, Center county. On an evening of July a detail of the soldiers, being at a little distance from the stockade, was attacked by a band of savages, and made a running fight for shelter. Two of the men were killed in sight of the fort, but their scalps were saved by a relief party. One of the Indians was killed and another severely wounded.

At Muncy a stockade fort had been built by Captain

---

3 Pennsylvania Archives, First Series, vol. vi., p. 660.

John Brady, the father of the famous Samuel, and there some of the bolder settlers had made a stand until the regulars came to their relief. John Brady had commanded a company in the Twelfth Pennsylvania, had been wounded at the battle of Brandywine, and had been honorably discharged from the continental service that he might assist in the defense of the northern frontier. Lieutenant Samuel Brady returned with his regiment to Muncy, and for the first time after three years of service in the army of the Revolution, was permitted to revisit his parents, brothers and sisters. The family reunion was not a long one. The Eighth Pennsylvania was relieved, at the end of July, by the Eleventh Pennsylvania, and Colonel Brodhead's men returned down the Susquehanna to Carlisle, arriving there on August 6.[4]

Before taking the road over the mountains to the West, the command rested at Carlisle one week. Just before it marched, Lieutenant Brady suffered a terrible blow. He received word that his younger brother James, from whom he had so recently parted, had been scalped by Indians and was dying at his home.

It was on Saturday, August 8, 1778, at the settlement of Peter Smith, about one mile below the site of Williamsport, on the bank of the West Branch, that James Brady received his mortal wounds.

On the preceding day 14 reapers and binders, accompanied by eight soldiers, went from Fort Brady to Smith's place to cut oats. The work of the first day was carried on without molestation. In the evening four of the men grew uneasy and went away. The morning of Saturday was very foggy. The cradlers began work at one side of the large field, under the protection of the soldiers. Six binders, of whom Brady was one, proceeded to the farther side of the field, separated from the view of the cradlers and soldiers by a ridge. Five of the binders placed their rifles against one tree, but Brady stood his apart.

---

4 Pennsylvania Archives, First Series, vol. vi., p. 680.

About an hour after sunrise, under cover of the fog, 30 Seneca and Muncy Indians slipped up on the binders and opened fire on them. The moment they were discovered Brady ran for his rifle, but the five other men took to their heels across the oatfield, leaving their guns untouched. Brady was shot and fell, but he sprang up, ran several rods, and fell again. Three Indians pounced upon him. He was wounded by a spear, struck on the head with a tomahawk and scalped. The soldiers and cradlers, hearing the firing, appeared on the ridge. The Indians exchanged a few shots with them, killing two of the white men, and then ran away into the forest. In the other direction the soldiers and the harvesters, with one exception, fled as rapidly toward Muncy.

The one exception was Jerome Veness. He discovered that young Brady was not dead, but was trying to make his way toward Smith's cabin, near the field. Veness assisted the wounded man into the cabin, and remained with him during the day, dressing his wounds as well as he was able. In the evening a company of soldiers reached Smith's plantation from Muncy. They made a rude litter and carried Brady on it to the house of his parents. There he lingered in a delirium for five days, but expired before his brother Samuel arrived from Carlisle.[5]

The Bradys were a family of vigorous bodies and strong passions. Samuel Brady's rage over the cruel death of his favorite brother was intense, and his soul was possessed with a craving for revenge. Tradition tells us that he ascertained that Bald Eagle, of the Wolf clan of the Delawares, and Cornplanter, a Seneca, were the chiefs of the Indian band and that he was relentless in his pursuit of those two savages, Brady had the satisfaction of killing Bald Eagle at the mouth of Red Bank creek, on the Allegheny, in June, 1779.[6] He was never able to accomplish the death of Cornplanter.

---

5 Pennsylvania Archives, First Series, vol. vi., pp. 688, 689, 691; Conquering the Wilderness, Triplett, New York, 1883, p. 213.

6 Pennsylvania Archives, First Series, vol. xii., p. 131; Washington-Irvine Correspondence, p. 41; William Young Brady, in Pittsburg Post, January 8, 1893.

Lieutenant Brady was excused, doubtless because of his brother's death, from accompanying the regiment on its march to Fort Pitt. During the month of September he was detailed as a recruiting officer in Cumberland county.

Before the Westmoreland regiment reached Fort Pitt it suffered another loss. Early in the year Captain Samuel Miller had been sent to Westmoreland county on the recruiting service. His home was about two miles northeast of the site of Greensburg. In July he was engaged, with several men of his company, in providing at Hannastown, near his home, a stock of forage and provisions for the coming regiment. On the 7th of July, while he and nine soldiers were conveying grain from a farm near the Kiskiminetas, they were waylaid and attacked by Indians, and only two of the white men escaped alive. The bodies of Captain Miller and his seven companions were afterward found, scalped and stripped.[7]

The Eighth regiment left Carlisle on August 13 and moved slowly.[8] It was two weeks going as far as Bedford, and two weeks more in making the journey over the mountains, past Ligonier and Hannastown, to Fort Pitt. It arrived at its destination, footsore and weary, on September 10, 1778, having been nearly three months on the road from the camp on the Schuylkill.[9] After it reached Bedford it was in its own country. From that place to Pittsburg, all along the line of march, there were many joyful reunions, and doubtless the travel-stained soldiers were well served with food and drink as they passed through Westmoreland. Yet many tearful women sat at the wayside cabins and sad-faced parents looked in vain for the familiar figures of beloved sons. Nearly three hundred of the stout frontier youths who marched away to the East to help Washington did not return to the defense of their own borderland.

---

[7] Pennsylvania Archives, First Series, vol. vi., p. 673; Frontier Forts, vol. ii., p. 323.

[8] Pennsylvania Archives, First Series, vol. vi., p. 700.

[9] Frontier Forts, vol. ii., p. 130.

CHAPTER XII.

THE ALLIANCE WITH THE DELAWARES.

The plan of General McIntosh for the protection of the frontier was to attack Detroit. In this he was encouraged by the opinions of many officers and members of Congress. The difficulty and hazard of such an undertaking was not appreciated in the East. It involved a march of more than 300 miles through a wilderness inhabited by savages, most of whom were hostile to the American cause. It must carry an army far from its base of supplies, and that base, at Fort Pitt, a precarious one. It was against an enemy having greater resources and a superior line of communication, by water, through Lakes Erie and Ontario. It was a project which Hand had meditated and which other commanders after McIntosh essayed; but all were doomed to disappointment.[1]

The two regiments of regulars, the Eighth Pennsylvania and the Thirteenth Virginia, were to be augmented by the militia from Westmoreland, and the three Virginia counties of Yohogania, Monongalia and Ohio, and there was hope of adding to these a force of Delaware warriors.

The Delawares, living on the Tuscarawas and the Muskingum, were the only Indians who had maintained neutrality between the Americans and the British. This was the tribe which had made the treaty with William Penn, under the elm at Shackamaxon, and its traditions attached it

---

1 Hand expressed the opinion that 3,000 men, with light artillery, would be necessary for the capture of Detroit. See Ft. Pitt, p. 229.

to the white man's council which sat at Philadelphia. Moreover, its head sachem, White Eyes, the greatest chieftain ever produced by this remarkable Indian nation, was peculiarly devoted to the American cause. He revealed a spirit of intelligent sympathy with the struggle for liberty, and even hoped that a Delaware Indian state might form a fourteenth star in the American Union.

Preparations were made to enter into a formal treaty of alliance with this Indian tribe. In June, 1778, Congress ordered the treaty to be held at Fort Pitt on July 23, and requested Virginia to name two commissioners and Pennsylvania one. Virginia chose General Andrew Lewis, the victor of Point Pleasant, and his brother, Thomas Lewis, a civilian; Pennsylvania neglected to appoint. It being found impossible for the continental troops to reach Pittsburg at the time first set, the treaty was postponed until September.

When Colonel Brodhead and his Westmoreland regulars marched into Fort Pitt, on September 10, 1778, they found the wigwams of the Delaware chiefs and warriors pitched near the shore of the Allegheny river, a short distance above the fort. Two days later, the conference between white men and red was begun in one of the buildings within the walls of Fort Pitt.

This was probably the most remarkable treaty ever made on behalf of the United States. Its proceedings are worthy of preservation as matters of curiosity and as illustrating one of the strange developments of the revolutionary struggle. They are handed down to us in the manuscript letter book of Colonel George Morgan, Indian agent at Fort Pitt.[2] By this treaty the United States entered into an offensive and defensive alliance with a tribe of savages, recognizing that tribe as an independent nation, guaranteeing its integrity and territory. Each party bound itself to assist the other against its enemies. The treaty laid the groundwork for the establishment of a system of judiciary

---

2 In the possession of the Pittsburg Carnegie Library.

THE ALLIANCE WITH THE DELAWARES. 75

in the Delaware nation and contained a provision for the admission of an Indian state into the American Union. The commissioners who made the treaty must have known that such a state was an impossibility, yet they deliberately provided for it in a solemn treaty, taking care, however, to subject the scheme to the approval of Congress. It was a "gold brick," presented by the white men to their red brethren.

It was a courageous act for the Delaware chiefs to form this alliance with the Americans. All other Indian tribes of the West were in league with the British, and for months had been coaxing and threatening the Delawares to draw them into the general combination. By daring to form an open union with the United States, White Eyes exposed his people to absolute destruction by the British and their red allies. He fully realized his danger, yet he had the courage to do what he believed to be the right thing. He fell a martyr to his convictions.

The Americans had sent messengers to the Shawnees, inviting them to come with the Delawares to the treaty, but that warlike tribe did not respond. The deputies of the Delawares were White Eyes, the chief sachem; Killbuck, a famous medicine man and war chief, and Pipe, the chief warrior of the Wolf clan. These three red men appeared at the council in holiday regalia, painted, feathered and beaded. Captain Pipe was especially celebrated for the gaudiness of his attire. The scene in the assembly room must have been picturesque. The councils were attended by General McIntosh and his colonels and staff officers, in new uniforms, and the Indian deputies were supported by a band of warriors in bright paint and gay blankets. The interpreter was Job Chilloway, a Delaware from the Susquehanna, who had lived many years among the white people.[3] Soldiers in hunting shirts patrolled before the barrack doors or stood in groups on the parade ground, watching the coming and going of the bedizened Indians.

---

[3] Morgan to the Delawares, August 12, 1778, MS. in Pittsburg Carnegie Library.

On the Saturday forenoon when the conference began, General Lewis offered the friendship of the United States and presented to the Indians a belt of white wampum, emblematic of peace. He praised the Delawares because they alone, of the many Indian tribes, had been faithful to their treaties; and in token of this fidelity he presented a broad belt of white wampum, having worked into it, in black, the figures of a white man and an Indian, connected by a black line, denoting a road or path. He then proposed a formal alliance, giving another white belt, showing a white man and an Indian clasping hands.

General Lewis stated the intention of sending an army against Detroit, and asked the permission of the Delawares for a passage through their territory. The Delawares claimed control over the country bounded on the east by the Allegheny and Ohio rivers, and on the west by the Hocking and Sandusky. Lewis expressed a desire that the western expedition might be so conducted as to cover and protect the Delaware towns in the Muskingum valley.

Chief White Eyes gave thanks for the offer of friendship and alliance. It was to form such an alliance that he and his comrades had come into council. He promised a prompt consultation and an answer in the afternoon. At this conference all the talking for the Indians was done by White Eyes. The speeches of this chief, on all occasions, were notable for their directness, force and clearness. He did not indulge in that metaphorical verbiage and tiresome prolixity by which Indian oratory is characterized. He had mingled much with white men, had studied their ways and imitated their style of speech.

In the afternoon there was no meeting, for another delegation of Indians arrived in camp, with firing of guns and beating of tom-toms, and the ceremonies of their reception occupied the time. They were led by Wingenund, the Delaware wise man, and by Nimwha, chief of a small band of Shawnees who lived with the Delawares at Coshocton.

It was on a fair Sunday that the conference was resumed. White Eyes announced the readiness of the Indians to accept the alliance. "We have taken fast hold of the chain of friendship," he said, "and are determined never to part the hold, though we should lose our lives." The commissioners then announcing that they would write out and submit the words of the treaty, White Eyes said: "Brothers, we are become one people. The enemy Indians, as soon as they hear it, will strike us. We desire that our brethren would build some place for our old men, women and children to remain in safety whilst our warriors go with you."

On Monday the articles of confederation between a civilized and a savage nation were interpreted and explained to the Indians. There was a heavy rainstorm on Tuesday, which prevented a meeting, but on Wednesday White Eyes accepted the treaty on behalf of the Delawares and the Maquegea branch of the Shawnees.

It was a momentous event in the life of this Indian chief and he delivered an affecting address, a brief outline of which has been preserved for us. "We now inform you," he said, "that as many of our warriors as can possibly be spared will join you and go with you." Thus he pronounced his own death warrant. "We are at a loss to express our thoughts, but we hope soon to convince you by our actions of the sincerity of our hearts. We desire you not to think any of our people will have any objection to your marching through our country; on the contrary, they will rejoice to see you."

He requested that Colonel John Gibson be appointed Indian agent, saying: "He has always acted an honest part by us, and we are convinced he will make our common good his chief study, and not think only how he may get rich." It appears that some of the Indian agents had the same weakness then as now.[4]

---

[4] This request of White Eyes was, of course, a reflection on Colonel Morgan, then Indian agent. Morgan was in Philadelphia at the time of the treaty and when he learned its terms he denounced it as improper and villainous. See Taylor's History of Ohio, Cincinnati, 1854, p. 291. Killbuck, who succeeded White Eyes as chief sachem of the Delawares, sent word to Morgan that he had not agreed with White Eyes in asking for the appointment of Gibson.

"When we were last in Philadelphia," White Eyes concluded, "our wise brethren in Congress may remember, we desired them to send a schoolmaster to our towns to instruct our children. As we think it will be for our mutual interest, we request it may be complied with."

The petitions of this wise Indian concerning Gibson and the schoolmaster were both neglected by the continental government.

On the following day, Thursday, September 17, 1778, the articles of confederation were signed in triplicate, one copy for Congress, one for the Delawares and one for General McIntosh. There were six articles, to the following effect: First, all offenses were to be mutually forgiven; second, a perpetual peace and friendship was pledged, each party to assist the other in any just war; third, the Delawares gave permission for the passage through their country of an American army, agreed to sell corn, meat and horses to that army, and to furnish guides and a body of warriors, while the United States bound themselves to erect and garrison, within the Delaware country, a fort for the protection of the old men, women and children; fourth, each party agreed to punish offenses committed by citizens of the other only by trial by judges or jurors of both parties, according to a system thereafter to be arranged; fifth, the United States pledged the establishment of a fair trade under the control of an honest agent.

The sixth article was the most remarkable. It guaranteed the integrity of the Delaware territory, so long as the nation should keep the peace with the United States, and concluded with the following provision, apparently drawn rather hastily:

"And it is further agreed on between the contracting parties that, should it, in future, be found conducive to the mutual interest of both parties, to invite any other tribe who have been friendly to the interest of the United States to join the present confederation and to form a state, whereof the Delaware nation shall be the head, and have a representative in Congress; provided nothing contained in this article be considered as conclusive until it meets with the approbation of Congress."

This is certainly as strange a proposition as ever was made to a savage nation. Of course, it never went any farther than the piece of parchment on which it was written. It was probably never intended to go any farther.

The treaty was signed by the several deputies, Andrew and Thomas Lewis, White Eyes, the Pipe and John Killbuck, the Indians making their marks. The following signatures were attached as those of witnesses: Lachlan McIntosh, Brigadier General, Commander of the Western Department; Daniel Brodhead, Colonel of the Eighth Pennsylvania Regiment; W. Crawford, Colonel; John Campbell, John Stephenson, John Gibson, Colonel of the Thirteenth Virginia Regiment; Arthur Graham, Brigade Major; Lachlan McIntosh, Jr., Brigade Major; Benjamin Mills, Joseph L. Finley, Captain of the Eighth Pennsylvania Regiment, and John Finley, Captain of the Eighth Pennsylvania Regiment.

On the succeeding day presents were given to the Delawares on behalf of Congress and the Indians then departed for Coshocton, to make preparations for joining the expedition against Detroit.

CHAPTER XIII.

FORT LAURENS.

In the notice of General McIntosh, in the "Dictionary of American Biography," is to be found this statement: "In a short time he restored peace to the frontier of Pennsylvania and Virginia." Unfortunately for the frontier, he did not do anything of the sort. He was as much a failure on the border as his predecessor, Hand, not because of his own lack of ability, but because of the want of men and supplies for the accomplishment of his plans. Immediately after the conclusion of the treaty with the Delawares, in the middle of September, 1778, McIntosh prepared to execute his design against Detroit. He had already summoned the militia from the frontier counties of Pennsylvania and Virginia. Westmoreland county failed to contribute, as her own borders were almost daily harried by savage bands. The Virginia counties, Yohogania, Monongalia and Ohio, furnished nearly 800 men, but they gathered at Fort Pitt slowly and provisions for the long campaign were collected with difficulty.

About October 1 the army, consisting of 1,300 men, of whom 500 were regulars of the Eighth Pennsylvania and the Thirteenth Virginia, moved from Fort Pitt down the Ohio, constructing a road along the southern bank of the river to the mouth of the Beaver.

Four weeks were occupied in the building of a fort on the high bluff overlooking the Ohio, on the western side of the Beaver river. The site of this fort was within the present town of Beaver, just above the station of the Cleveland and Pittsburg railroad. It was built under the direction of Colonel Cambray, a French engineer and chief of the artillery in McIntosh's army. The walls were of heavy logs, filled in with earth, and on them six-pound cannon were mounted. The fort contained barracks for a regiment of soldiers. The commander designed Fort McIntosh as an advanced depot for munitions and provisions. It was the most western point to which supplies could be conveyed with ease by water, but from the mouth of the Beaver onward the expedition must go entirely by land.[1]

While Fort McIntosh was building, the general was trying to get forward his stores, in preparation for the march into the wilderness. But things moved slowly over the bad roads of the frontier. Every delay was annoying to the Scotch commander. The fine days of autumn were slipping by and Detroit was still far away. The Delaware Indians, of whom a band of 60 warriors accompanied the army, could not understand why so much time was spent in building a fort which would not be needed when Detroit was captured, and some of the American officers considered the month passed at the mouth of the Beaver as that much time wasted.

On November 3 a herd of lean cattle, driven over the mountains, arrived at Fort McIntosh, and two days later the army began its march westward through the Indian country. The pack horses and cattle were so poor and weak that they could not make more than five or six miles a day, and it was November 19 when the force reached the Tuscarawas river, at the site of the present town of Bolivar, near the line between Stark and Tuscarawas counties.

According to the pledge contained in the treaty with the Delawares, to erect a fort in their country for the protection of their women and children, it was the intention of General McIntosh to build a stockade at the Delaware capital of Coshocton, at the junction of the Tuscarawas and the

---

[1] Fort McIntosh and Its Times, monograph by Daniel Agnew; Washington-Irvine Correspondence, p. 23, etc.

Walhonding, but several things conspired to thwart this plan.² During the march to the Tuscarawas the Delaware chief, White Eyes, was "treacherously put to death." The exact manner of his killing is unknown, but it is believed that he was shot by a Virginia militiaman.³ His death caused dismay among his warriors and most of them deserted the American force and returned to Coshocton. It became thereafter uncertain whether the Americans would be received kindly at the Delaware capital. A march south to Coshocton would take the army far out of its way. Beyond all, the season had now become so late that Detroit was out of the question. A winter campaign through the land of the savages was not to be considered.

With great reluctance McIntosh was driven to the conclusion that he could not continue his campaign during that season. He was not willing, however, to retire without accomplishing something. He decided to build a stockade fort at Tuscarawas, where the army was then encamped, to hold that place during the winter and from it to set forth in the spring on another attempt against Detroit. Such a fort would fulfill the pledge of the treaty to build a place of refuge in the Delaware country, and McIntosh hoped to send out war parties from it to strike the towns on the Sandusky river. Even this hope was ruined by the general's failure to bring forward sufficient provisions.

The fort at the Tuscarawas was built on the west bank of the river, about half a mile below the present village of Bolivar. It was a small thing, enclosing only about an acre of ground. High embankments of earth were raised and topped with pickets, consisting of logs set upright and pointed at the top. Colonel Cambray superintended the building of this fort, which was named Laurens, after the president of the Continental Congress.⁴

While this work was going on, McIntosh found that he could not get forward sufficient provisions to maintain

---

2 Ft. Pitt, p. 234.
3 Crumrine's History of Washington County, Pa., note on p. 220.
4 Albach's Western Annals, p. 300; Pennsylvania Archives, First Series, vol. vii., p. 131.

his large force in the Indian country long enough even for an expedition against the Sandusky towns. The commissary department seems to have been managed miserably, although it contended with great difficulties.[5]

The time of the Virginia militia ran only until the end of the year. The weather began to grow cold, and to prevent starvation and disaster in the snows, McIntosh was forced to return with his army to the Ohio. He left at Fort Laurens 150 men of the Thirteenth Virginia, under Colonel John Gibson, the stout-hearted and active frontiersman. Colonel Brodhead, with a detachment of the Eighth Pennsylvania, formed the winter garrison of Fort McIntosh, while General McIntosh took up his quarters in Fort Pitt, and there brooded over his disappointments.

A terrible winter was spent by the little garrison of Fort Laurens. Colonel Gibson did not have sufficient food to last him until spring, and hunting in the woods was soon stopped by the appearance of hostile Indians. The savages began to prowl about the post early in January, 1779. The erection of this fort, almost in the heart of the Indian country, greatly provoked the savages of the Wyandot, Miami and Mingo tribes, and they plotted its destruction.[6]

McIntosh had promised to send back provisions, and about the middle of January Captain John Clark, of the Eighth Pennsylvania, was sent from Fort McIntosh with 15 men to convoy pack horses, with flour and meat, to the little post on the Tuscarawas.

Captain Clark reached the fort in safety on January 21 and two days later set out on his return to the Ohio. Three miles from the fort he was ambushed by Simon Girty and 17 Mingo Indians, who killed two of the soldiers, wounded four and captured one.[7] Captain Clark was driven back to the fort, but a few days afterward he again started and went

---
5 Frontier Forts, vol. ii., p. 489; Pennsylvania Archives, First Series, vol. viii., pp. 109, 405.
6 Zeisberger to Morgan, January 20, 1779, MS. in Pittsburg Carnegie Library.
7 Pennsylvania Archives, First Series, vol. vii., p. 173.

through without molestation. Girty carried his prisoner to Detroit, where he raised a much larger force and returned to the vicinity of Fort Laurens.

About the middle of February the wilderness post was surrounded by a band of 200 Indians, mostly Miamis and Mingoes, led by Captain Henry Bird and Girty.[8] Gibson succeeded in sending a messenger through the savage lines, who carried the news of the situation to General McIntosh, with this word from Gibson:

"You may depend upon my defending the fort to the last extremity."

On February 23 the garrison suffered a severe loss. Early in the winter the men had cut a lot of firewood and piled it in the forest not far from the fort. On the day mentioned a wagon was sent out, under an escort of 18 soldiers, to haul some of the wood into the stockade. At about half a mile from the fort the little party passed by an ancient Indian mound, and behind that mound a band of savages lay hidden. As the white men went along one side of the mound the Indians burst upon them, both in front and rear, took them completely by surprise and quickly killed and scalped every member of the party except two, who were taken prisoners.

The Indians now laid regular siege to the fort and endeavored to starve it into surrender. The camp fires of the savages were seen at night in the bleak woods, and in the daytime the warriors showed themselves on the adjacent hills, shaking their guns at the fort and waving aloft the scalps of the slain soldiers. The food of the garrison grew so scanty that Colonel Gibson cut down the daily ration to a quarter of a pound of flour and the same weight of meat. Gibson sent another messenger for help, a courageous fellow, who eluded the watchful Indians and reached Fort McIntosh on March 3. At once the general set about to gather a relieving force, but it was two weeks before he collected enough men to do any good.

---

8 The Westward Movement, Justin Winsor, p. 138; The Girtys, p. 94.

In the meantime the straits of the garrison grew desperate. A sortie in force was contemplated, but this was given up when a count was made of the besieging savages. The Indians paraded over the crest of a hill within plain sight of the garrison, and about 850 warriors were counted. This kept the garrison closely within the walls. It was learned years afterward that there were not more than 200 Indians, but they had exaggerated their real strength by marching around the farther base of the hill and showing themselves in long single file, four or five times over, within sight of the white men.

Captain Bird, after this stratagem, sent in a demand for surrender, promising safe passage for the soldiers to Fort McIntosh, but Gibson sternly refused. The Indians then promised to withdraw if Gibson would furnish them with a barrel of flour and a barrel of meat. Bird believed that the garrison was reduced to its last provisions and would refuse the request. In such an event, he felt certain that starvation would bring the white men to terms in a few days. Gibson had but a few barrels of food, and that in bad condition, but he quickly complied with the demand, sent out the two barrels and said that he had plenty left. The savages were discouraged, for they were almost without food themselves. The snow was so deep that they were not able to replenish their larder. They had a feast on the flour and pork, and on the following day left the vicinity and returned to their towns in Northwestern Ohio.

On March 23 General McIntosh appeared with his relieving force of 300 regulars and 200 militiamen, escorting a train of pack horses with provisions. The joy of the garrison was excessive. For more than a week the men had been living on roots and soup made by boiling rawhides.

The famished men sallied forth with their rifles and fired a volley to express their gladness. The shooting frightened the pack horses and they stampeded through the woods, scattering their provisions in every direction. Some of the horses were never recovered and not more than half of the food was gathered up.

General McIntosh remained only two or three days at Fort Laurens. Colonel Gibson and his hungry Virginians were relieved and returned with the general to Fort Pitt, while Major Vernon and 100 men of the Eighth Pennsylvania were subsituted as the garrison of the wilderness post.

In February, before going to the relief of Fort Laurens, General McIntosh had concluded that he was a failure as a frontier officer, and had written to General Washington asking to be recalled. The Commander-in-Chief acceded to the request, with evident chagrin, and named Colonel Daniel Brodhead, of the Eighth Pennsylvania, as commander of the Western Department. The nomination of Brodhead was communicated to Congress on March 5 and was approved by that body. On his return to Fort Pitt, April 3, McIntosh received the notification of his release from command, and soon afterward departed for Philadelphia, while Colonel Brodhead went from Fort McIntosh to Fort Pitt and took charge of affairs.[9]

In writing of McIntosh, under date of February 20, 1779, General Washington said: "I wish matters had been more prosperously conducted under the command of General McIntosh. This gentleman was in a manner a stranger to me, but during the time of his residence at Valley Forge I had imbibed a good opinion of his good sense, attention to duty and disposition to correct public abuses, qualifications much to be valued in a separate and distinct command. To these considerations were added (and not the least) his disinterested concern with respect to the disputes which had divided and distracted the inhabitants of that western world, and which would have rendered an officer from either Pennsylvania or Virginia improper, while no one could be spared from another state with so much convenience as McIntosh. He is now coming away, and the second in command, Brodhead (as there will be no military operations of consequence to be conducted), will

---

9 Washington-Irvine Correspondence, p. 35.

succeed him. But once for all, it may not be amiss for me to conclude with this observation, that, with such means as are provided, I must labor."[10]

Brodhead was one of the officers who believed that the building of Fort McIntosh was useless and the erection of Fort Laurens foolish. During April and May the soldiers in Fort Laurens, though free from serious Indian attacks, suffered great privations through the shortage of food. A few deer were killed by Delaware Indian hunters and sold to the garrison, but in the middle of May Brodhead ordered the greater part of the force to return to Fort McIntosh to escape actual starvation. Major Vernon remained with only 25 men until August 1, part of the time being reduced for food to herbs, salt and boiled hides. It was impossible to keep the place provisioned so far in the wilderness. The fort was finally dismantled, by Brodhead's orders, and the last little handful of men returned to Fort Pitt. The stockade remained for many years, falling into decay slowly. Fifty years ago some of the pickets were standing, and even now the outlines of the embankments can be made out on the western bank of the Tuscarawas river.[11]

---

10 Magazine of American History, vol. iii., p. 132.
11 Historical Collections of Ohio, vol. ii., p. 693.

CHAPTER XIV.

SAMUEL BRADY'S REVENGE.

General Washington excused the appointment of Colonel Brodhead to the command of the Western Department on the plea that no important operations were to be undertaken in that quarter. Brodhead did not understand the matter in that light. He had his own ideas about the defense of the frontier and proceeded actively to put them into execution; and although not much was expected of him, he proved to be the most vigorous and the most successful in punishing the savages among all the commanders at Fort Pitt during the Revolution, including his two successors as well as two predecessors.

In the beginning of April, 1779, McIntosh transferred to Brodhead 722 men, regulars and militia.[1] Most of these troops were at Forts Pitt and McIntosh, but small parties garrisoned Fort Henry, at Wheeling; Fort Randolph, at Point Pleasant, and Fort Hand, near the Kiskiminetas, three and a half miles southwest of the site of Apollo. About the middle of April, Lieutenant Lawrence Harrison, formerly one of Gibson's Lambs, but now connected with the Thirteenth Virginia, was sent to occupy Fort Crawford, a small stockade built by Colonel William Crawford at Parnassus, during the preceding summer. Forts Hand and Crawford were intended to protect the northern border of Westmoreland county from the raids of the Iroquois who

---

[1] Pennsylvania Archives, First Series, vol. xii., p. 106; Frontier Forts, vol. ii., p. 327.

lived on the upper waters of the Allegheny river, but they were not altogether effective.

With the first mild weather of spring the incursions of the savages began. The Senecas and Muncys descended the Allegheny in canoes until within striking distance of the Westmoreland settlements, hid their canoes in the thickets and scattered in little bands through the country. They burned cabins, killed and scalped the men, carried off the women, children and household goods, regained their canoes and ascended the river before they could be overtaken by the soldiers or aroused settlers. It was almost impossible for regular troops to accomplish anything in this kind of predatory warfare. The movements of the Indians were secret and swift. Except when snow was on the ground, they usually left no trail that could be followed save by the most experienced woodsman. The spring and early summer of 1779 present a terrible record of Indian depredations on the border, and the northern portion of Westmoreland county, between the Forbes road (nearly the present line of the Pennsylvania railroad) and the Kiskiminetas river, was almost depopulated.

Brodhead put into operation a system of scouting along the border, from one fort to another, and from the regulars at Fort Pitt he organized a number of ranging bands, composed of the boldest and most experienced frontiersmen, whom he sent on extended tours into the forests. To command these ranging parties he selected three of the bravest and keenest woodsmen in the Eighth Pennsylvania, Captain Van Swearingen, Lieutenant Samuel Brady and Lieutenant John Hardin. It was in this work that Brady won fame as an Indian fighter and killer.

Daniel Boone said, in his elder days, that, while he had fought Indians for many years, he did not know positively that he had ever killed one. Such was not the case with Samuel Brady. His hatred of the red men was personal and he made it his business to kill them. He had abundant justification. The cruel death of his brother, in August, 1778, was followed by the killing of his father, Captain John Brady, on April 11, 1779. Captain Brady was conveying supplies from Fort Wallis to Muncy, on the west branch of the Susquehanna, when he was shot dead from his horse by three Iroquois Indians secreted in a thicket. His body was recovered unscalped and was buried at Muncy, where a handsome monument was erected by public subscription in 1879.[2] Samuel Brady received news of his father's death about the time he was chosen by Brodhead as a forest ranger. It swelled his hatred of the Indian race, gave him additional eagerness on the warpath and nerved his arm to execute vengeance.

Only a brief review is possible of the Indian depredations in Westmoreland county in that terrible spring of 1779. On April 15 Colonel Brodhead wrote to a friend in the East, "The Indians are daily committing murders in Westmoreland to such a degree that it is apprehended they have formed a camp on some of the waste lands of the inhabitants." Toward the end of April a strong band of Iroquois entered the Ligonier settlement, slaughtered cattle and hogs, killed one man and carried two families into captivity.[3]

It was probably the same band, estimated to be 100 strong and accompanied by several tories, that attacked Fort Hand on April 26. The garrison consisted of 17 men, under Captain Samuel Moorhead and Lieutenant William Jack. About 1 o'clock in the afternoon the savages fired from the woods at two ploughmen, who escaped unharmed into the stockade. The team of horses and the yoke of oxen with which they were working were killed by the Indians, who then spread around the place and shot down all the domestic animals in sight. The savages hid behind stumps, fences and sheds and opened fire on the fort, which was returned with vigor by the garrison. Several women within the stockade molded bullets for the riflemen, and the firing kept up briskly until nightfall. Three members of

---

2 Meginness's History of the West Branch; Notes and Queries, vol. i., p. 123.

3 Pennsylvania Archives, First Series, vol. vii., p. 345.

the garrison were wounded and one of them died a few days later. He was Sergeant Philip McGraw, who occupied a sentry box in a corner bastion. A bullet entered a narrow porthole, and after McGraw had been shot and removed, a man of the name of McCauley was wounded in the same manner.

During the night the Indians continued to whoop and shoot at the stockade. They mimicked the sentinel's cry, "All's well!" About midnight the savages set fire to John McKibben's large log house not far from the fort, and as the flames poured upward and illuminated the stockade, the tories among the Indians cried, "Is all well now?" There was but little wind and the fire did not spread. In the morning the savages were still about the fort, but during the forenoon they gave up the siege and went away to the northward. During the night a messenger had been sent out and he made his way to Fort Pitt for aid. Forty soldiers were hurried to Fort Hand, but they were too late to intercept the marauders.[4]

During May Brodhead kept his scouts out along the upper Allegheny, to give warning of the approach of any other hostile bands, and he was employing every exertion to prepare for an expedition into the Seneca country. He was much hampered by the lack of supplies, which came with painful slowness over the mountain roads from the East. For many days his men were without meat. Flour was bought only at a high price. The soldiers were clothed in rags and many were without shoes. They learned to make Indian moccasins, and Brady and his scouts were clad almost entirely in the Indian fashion. On all their forest excursions they painted their bodies and faces as the savages did, wore feathers in their long hair and were to be distinguished only by close scrutiny from the red men whom they hunted. They were accompanied by a few Delaware warriors, who rendered excellent service in trailing the Seneca war parties. A young Delaware chief, Nanowland,

---

4 Washington-Irvine Correspondence, p. 39; Pennsylvania Archives, First Series, vol. vii., p. 362; Frontier Forts, vol. ii., p. 328.

took an especial fancy to Brady and was with him so constantly as to become known as Brady's "Pet Indian."

About the first of June Brodhead was informed that a large band of Seneca Indians and tories, under Colonel John Butler, was preparing to descend the Allegheny river and ravage the settlements. He sent three scouts in a canoe up the Allegheny as far as Venango (the present Franklin). There they were discovered by a party of hostile Indians, who pursued them in canoes almost to the mouth of the Kiskiminetas. The scouts had a narrow escape and the news they brought to Fort Pitt satisfied Brodhead that the threatened invasion was at hand.

The savages were not as numerous, however, as was supposed. There were but seven of them. They hid their canoes on the Allegheny and penetrated into Westmoreland county between Fort Hand and Fort Crawford. There they encountered a solitary soldier, and left him dead and scalped in the woods. They surprised the little settlement at James Perry's mill, on Big Sewickley creek, killed a woman and four children and carried off two children, half a dozen horses, blankets, jewelry and articles of female raiment.[5]

When the news of this raid reached Fort Pitt two parties were sent out after the Indians. One considerable company marched to the Sewickley settlement and attempted from there to follow the Indian trail. The other band, consisting of 20 men under Brady, all painted and dressed like Indians, ascended the Allegheny river. Brady was satisfied that the marauders came from the north and would return in that direction, regain their hidden canoes and seek to escape by water. His experience told him that the surest way to cut them off would be to make a rapid march up the stream. His men kept a sharp lookout for the Indian canoes and toward an evening found them drawn up amid shrubbery, on the beach within the mouth of one of the large creeks entering the Allegheny from the east. The

---

5 Pennsylvania Archives, First Series, vol. vii., p. 505.

authorities differ as to the identity of this creek. McCabe, who compiled a series of traditions concerning Brady's exploits, says that it was the Big Mahoning. Colonel Brodhead. in his contemporary report to General Washington, says that it was "about 15 miles above Kittanning." This agrees with the location of Red Bank creek, and would make the scene of Brady's adventure not far from the place since called Brady's Bend.

The Indians had gone into camp in the woods, on a little knoll north of the creek, and were preparing their evening meal when discovered by Brady. They had hobbled the stolen horses and turned them out to graze on the meadow between their camp and the creek. This stream was very high and the scouts were compelled to ascend it two miles before they were able to wade across.

After nightfall Brady and his men stealthily descended the northern side of the creek until they were near the Indian camp, and hid themselves in the tall grass of the meadow. Crawling on their stomachs, they approached closer and closer to the hill where the Indians and their prisoners were sleeping around the campfire. They were much annoyed by the horses in the meadow, which threatened to betray the presence of the strange creatures in the grass, but the animals were probably too weary with their long journey of the day to make any demonstrations of alarm.

Brady and Nanowland, laying aside their tomahawks, knives, powder horns and bullet pouches, crept to within a few yards of the Indian camp, to count the savages and ascertain the position of the captive children. One of the Indian warriors suddenly cast off his blanket, arose, stepped forth to within six feet of where Brady lay, stood there awhile, stretched himself and then returned to his slumber. Brady and Nanowland then crawled silently back to their companions and prepared for an attack at daybreak.

The whole party of scouts made their way amid the grass and bushes as near the Indian camp as was considered safe, and lay awaiting the dawn. By and by, as morning began to come, one Indian awoke and aroused the others. They stood about the fire, laughing and chatting, when a deadly volley blazed forth from the adjacent bushes. The chief of the seven Indians fell dead and the others fled almost naked into the dense forest, two of them being severely wounded. Brady's own rifle brought down the Indian captain, and, with a shout of almost fiendish triumph, Brady sprang forward and scalped the fallen chief. The traditions of the Brady family say that this chief was the very Indian, Bald Eagle, who had struck down and scalped Brady's younger brother on the Susquehanna ten months before. Brodhead informed Washington that he was "a notorious warrior of the Muncy nation."

The two wounded Indians were trailed for some distance by the drops of blood on the ground, but they quickly staunched their wounds with leaves and were lost in the dense thickets. Nanowland uttered the cry of a young wolf, the peculiar call of the Muncys, and it was twice answered by the fugitives; but further calls brought no response and the wounded savages could not be found. Three weeks later Brady was in the same neighborhood and observed a flock of crows hovering about a thicket. On searching there, he found the partially devoured body of an Indian.[6]

The children captured at Sewickley were recovered unharmed and Brady and his men returned to Fort Pitt with the stolen horses and plunder, the blankets, guns, tomahawks and knives of the savages. The punishment of this Indian band was so severe that not another inroad was made by the northern savages into Westmoreland county during that year.

---

6 Pennsylvania Archives, First Series, vol. xii., p. 131; Washington-Irvine Correspondence, p. 41; Hist. Coll. of Pa., p. 99.

CHAPTER XV.

BRODHEAD'S RAID UP THE ALLEGHENY.

The raids on the Pennsylvania and Virginia frontier in 1778 were made by the Indians of the Ohio country; those of 1779 by the Senecas and Muncys of the North, from the upper tributaries and headwaters of the Allegheny. The western tribes were temporarily disorganized by Clark's capture of Hamilton, the governor of Detroit, at Vincennes, in February, 1779, and by a destructive raid made by Kentuckians on the Shawnee towns on the Scioto, in May, 1779.

The Seneca tribe of Western New York was the largest of the Six Nations. Its warriors were second only to the Mohawks in courage and military prowess. Under Cornplanter, Guyasuta and other war captains they distressed a wide extent of country in New York and Pennsylvania and decorated their huts in the valley of the Genesee with the scalps of hundreds of white persons.

It was to these marauders that Colonel Brodhead directed his attention, and he begged General Washington for permission to lead an expedition into the Seneca land. Early in the summer the Commander-in-Chief directed the formation of a large army under General John Sullivan, to invade the Iroquois territory from the east, and about the middle of July Colonel Brodhead received permission from General Washington to undertake a movement of co-operation up the Allegheny valley.[1]

---
1 See Brodhead's Letter Book in Pennsylvania Archives, First Series, vol. xii., Brodhead to County Lieutenants, July 17, 1779; Brodhead to Bayard, July 20, 1779; Brodhead to Washington, July 31, 1779.

Amid great difficulty Brodhead acted promptly, for he was prepared to depart from Fort Pitt within four weeks from the time he received Washington's letter. He had been making preparations for such an expedition ever since he took command of the department. Workmen from Philadelphia had built 60 boats, some in the form of large skiffs and others hollowed out of great poplar logs. Extra provisions had been slowly collected, more than 200 pack-horses were ready, and a large drove of live cattle had been brought over the mountains. In June Lieutenant Colonel Bayard built a stockade at Kittanning, which was called Fort Armstrong, after General John Armstrong, of Carlisle. This served as a sort of way-station on the march. The last remnant of the garrison of Fort Laurens, on the Tuscarawas, came into Fort Pitt early in August and Colonel Brodhead was then ready to proceed.[2]

The expedition left Pittsburg on August 11, 1779. It numbered 605 men. Small garrisons of regulars were left in Forts McIntosh, Pitt, Crawford and Armstrong. A part of the force consisted of militiamen and volunteers from the surrounding country, to whom Brodhead had promised a share of the plunder. A small band of Delawares accompanied the expedition, and acted with the scouting parties under Brady and Hardin.

The flour, liquors and other provisions were conveyed by boats up the Allegheny river as far as the mouth of the Big Mahoning. The main body marched along the eastern bank, past Forts Crawford and Armstrong. The cattle followed under a strong guard. Amid these conditions progress was necessarily slow. When the army reached the mouth of the Mahoning, a heavy rain set in and continued for four days. Tents were insufficient to shelter the whole force. The men suffered great discomfort, and many were afflicted with rheumatism. The supplies were taken from the boats and loaded on the horses, and when the rain ceased the expedition proceeded under most unfavorable conditions.

---

2 Brodhead's Report to Washington, Pennsylvania Archives, vol. xii., p. 155; Mag. of Amer. History, vol. iii., p. 649.

At this point the army left the river, which flows down from the northwest, and followed an Indian trail which ran almost due north through the forest wilderness of what is now Clarion county. The use of this path stretched out the army into a long, thin line, whose weakness was covered by the scouts, kept well out in front and on flank. This trail was so bad that on the return Brodhead preferred another route. Even now the country is a rough one. The woods were full of broken timber, and many swollen streams were forded.

The trail crossed the Tionesta near its mouth and returned to the Allegheny river at the site of an old Indian town which Brodhead called Cushcushing. This is a Delaware name, more accurately written Quoshquoshink, and means Place of Hogs. It had for a few years been deserted, but was marked by the ruins of the Indian huts. It was not far from the present town of Tionesta.[3]

At Cushcushing the troops crossed the Allegheny river to the right bank and pushed on toward the mouth of Brokenstraw creek. At that place there had been an Indian town called Buckaloons, but this was known to be deserted. Brodhead hoped, however, to strike the Senecas at their village of Conewago, at the mouth of what is now called Conewango creek, where Warren has been built.[4]

A few miles below the Brokenstraw, the expedition had its only fight with the savages. It was near Thompson, a station on the Western New York & Pennsylvania railroad, where there is an island in the Allegheny river. In that neighborhood the river hills are high and so close to

---

[3] This Indian village site has sometimes been confused with Kuskuskee, at the fork of the Beaver river. Quashquoshink was visited by Rev. David Zeisberger, the Moravian missionary, in 1767, and he dwelt there for two years. The villagers were notorious for their immorality and debauchery, and were probably of the Wolf clan of Delawares. See Loskiel's History of the Moravian Mission. General Irvine, who surveyed this region in 1785, located "Cuskushing" 25 miles up the Allegheny from the mouth of French creek. Pennsylvania Archives, First Series, vol. xi., p. 516.

[4] The stream then called Conewago is now Conewango and is the outlet of Chautauqua Lake. Conewago is the same word as Caughnewago, used to designate an Indian village near Montreal and a mixed band of Indians living in northern Ohio.

the stream, that there are, in some places, very narrow passes. It was in one of these passes that the encounter took place.[5]

Lieutenant Hardin was in advance, with 15 white scouts and eight Delaware Indians, when they discovered, coming down the river, seven canoes, containing more than 30 Seneca warriors. The captain of this war party, on its way to raid the settlements, may have been Guyasuta. Tradition has assigned the command to Cornplanter, but at that time Cornplanter was in the Genesee country, trying to withstand the advance of Sullivan's army. Each party observed the other at almost the same moment. The Senecas at once ran their canoes to shore, threw off their shirts and prepared for battle. The Indians always entered a conflict as nearly naked as possible. The boldness with which the savages prepared for the fray shows that they did not believe their opponents to be numerous. They would never have prepared for the fight in this manner had they suspected the presence of a large force.

Both sides took to trees and rocks and began a sharp fusillade. For only a few minutes this conflict lasted, when another party of scouts, moving over the hills, took the Senecas in flank and poured down a hot fire upon them. At the sound of the firing in front Brodhead formed his column so as to protect the pack-train and then hurried forward with reinforcements. He was just in time to witness the retreat of the Senecas. They quickly discovered that they were overpowered and took to rapid flight. Some of them leaped into the river and waded and swam across. The shooting of the scouts was so accurate that the savages dared not pause on the shore to push off their canoes. Most of the Indians escaped along the bank and were soon out of sight amid the trees and thickets.

Five dead Indians lay on the field. Several others had

---

5 Brodhead said, in his report, that the fight took place "ten miles this side the town," meaning ten miles below Conewago or Warren. Not being acquainted with the country, his estimate of the distance was not likely to be accurate. Thompson's station, supposed to be the site of the skirmish, is about fourteen miles below Warren.

gone away wounded, leaving trails of blood. Eight of their guns were left behind, as well as their seven canoes, containing their blankets, shirts and provisions. Only three of Brodhead's men were wounded, and they so slightly that they continued on the march the following morning. One of the wounded was Jonathan Zane, the Wheeling scout and guide, who received a nip in the arm, and the two others were Nanowland, the young Delaware chief, and Joseph Nicholson, the interpreter.

The army went into camp near the scene of conflict, and on the following morning moved up to the Brokenstraw. Here Brodhead decided to leave his stores and baggage and march light to Conewago. A rude breastwork, guarded by fallen trees and bundles of fagots, was constructed on a high bluff commanding an extensive view up and down the river. A captain and 40 men remained in charge, and the expedition pushed on for Conewago. There Brodhead was disappointed by finding the Iroquois town deserted and the huts falling to decay. This was as far as his guides were acquainted with the country, but the commander determined to follow an Indian trail which led over the hills toward the northeast.

After a march of 20 miles the troops came again within sight of the Allegheny river, and from a hilltop discovered a number of Indian villages, surrounded by great fields of splendid corn and patches of beans, squashes and melons. This Iroquois settlement extended for eight miles along the fertile bottom land of the Allegheny river, where the Cornplanter reservation was afterward established.

The soldiers hurriedly descended into the villages, but found that all the houses were deserted. The Indian spies had discovered the approach of the Americans, and the warriors had fled so hurriedly with their women and children that they had left behind many deer skins and other articles of value.

The Iroquois had long before this learned to build substantial log houses, even squaring the timbers as the white pioneers did. In this Allegheny river settlement there were about 130 houses, some of them being large enough for three or four families. In the uppermost village stood a great war post, painted and decorated with dog skins, and that village was evidently the dwelling place of the chief.

In his report to Washington, Brodhead wrote: "The troops remained on the ground three whole days, destroying the towns and corn fields. I never saw finer corn, although it was planted much thicker than is common with our farmers. The quantity of corn and vegetables destroyed at the several towns, from the best accounts I can collect from the officers employed to destroy it, must certainly exceed 500 acres, which is the lowest estimate, and the plunder taken is estimated at $3,000. From the great quantity of corn in the ground and the number of new houses built and building, it appears that the whole Seneca and Muncy nations intended to collect in this settlement."

On the return march the supplies were picked up at Buckaloons, and the troops marched across country to French creek. At Oil creek the soldiers rubbed themselves freely with the oil which they found floating on the water, and received great relief from their rheumatic pains and stiffness. For many years this petroleum was called Seneca oil, and was supposed to be valuabale only for its medicinal qualities. The army reached French creek at the mouth of Conneaut creek, where the Muncy town of Maghingue-chahocking was found to be deserted. It was composed of 35 large huts, which were burnend. The Muncys formed a branch of the Wolf clan of the Delawares, and had long lived and associated with the Iroquois. Their reputation as thieves, murderers and general reprobates was very bad.

The army descended French creek almost to its mouth and thence returned to Fort Pitt by what is known as the Venango path. This was an old Indian trail running almost due north and south through the heart of Butler county. It crossed Slippery Rock and Connoquenessing creeks, and came down to the Allegheny river along the course of

Pine creek. It was a much more direct route than that followed by the troops in marching northward, along the course of the Allegheny river.

It is said that Slippery Rock creek received its name from an accident that occurred during this return march. The troops crossed the creek at a point where the bed of the stream is composed of smooth, level rock, like a floor. On this the horse of John Ward slipped and fell and severely injured the rider.

The expedition arrived at Fort Pitt on September 14, without the loss of a single man or horse. In summing up the results, Brodhead wrote: "I have a happy presage that the counties of Westmoreland, Bedford and Northumberland, if not the whole western frontier, will experience the good effect of it. Too much praise cannot be given to both officers and soldiers of every corps during the whole expedition. Their perseverance and zeal during the whole (through a country too inaccessible to be described) can scarcely be equaled in history."

The thanks of Congress were voted to Colonel Brodhead, and in a general order, issued on October 18, General Washington said: "The activity, perseverance and firmness which marked the conduct of Colonel Brodhead, and that of all the officers and men of every description in this expedition, do them great honor, and their services entitle them to the thanks and to this testimonial of the General's acknowledgment."

CHAPTER XVI.

THE WINTER OF THE DEEP SNOW.

A winter and a summer, each remarkable in its way, followed the expedition of Brodhead to the upper Allegheny. These seasons were known as "the winter of the deep snow" and "the summer of the big harvest." The soldiers and settlers on the frontier were much indebted to the character of that winter for their immunity from Indian raids. It bound their enemies, but also afflicted them. Hunger and cold are probably preferable, however, to the torch, the rifle and the scalping knife of the savage.

While the incursions to the Seneca country had much to do with checking the savage inroads in the autumn, the border was poorly prepared for defense during the winter. The Indian raids of the spring and summer of 1779 had interfered with sowing and reaping, and there was small surplus of food in the barns and cellars of the settlers. A quarrel in the autumn between Colonel Brodhead and the militia officers of Westmoreland county prevented co-operation on any system for guarding the border. Had the ensuing season been an open one, Westmoreland county would have been devastated. During the 12 months beginning with November, 1779, the influence of the weather on human affairs was strongly manifested.

Both Colonel Brodhead, the regular officer in command of the Western Department, and Archibald Lochry, the county lieutenant of Westmoreland, claimed authority over the two companies of rangers formed in Westmoreland. On the approach of winter, Brodhead ordered these two companies to evacuate Forts Armstrong and Crawford, where they lacked supplies and clothing, and join the regulars at Fort Pitt. Lochry ordered them to Hannastown, that he might post them along the line of the Kiskiminetas river. Much time was wasted by the dispute, but Lochry showed that he had authority to direct the movements of the rangers except in times of aggressive action, and they marched to Hannastown. Then Brodhead, in a fit of pique, refused to provide the rangers with food and ammunition, although they were in the continental service. Lochry had no supplies for them, and he was forced to quarter them, in little parties of four and five, at the houses of the principal settlers. These settlers were willing to feed the men out of their slender stores, rather than lose their protection.[1]

The winter of 1779-80 began early and continued until March. It was perhaps the severest winter in the history of the United States. In January the harbor of New York was frozen over so solidly that the British drove laden wagons on the ice from the city to Staten Island. In Western Pennsylvania the snow began to fall heavily about the holidays and was followed by exceedingly cold weather for two months.

The snow accumulated at intervals, and by February 1 was four feet deep in the woods and on the mountains. This stopped all the supply trains from the East, and the garrison at Fort Pitt suffered severely for food and clothing. Many of the soldiers were without shoes, and scouting expeditions were out of the question. The officers were without money or credit, and were reduced to extreme straits. Delaware Indians, who visited the fort in the fall, clung to it all winter, and seem to have found whisky easier to procure than bread.[2]

---

1 For Brodhead's quarrels with the frontier officers and for other facts narrated in this chapter, see the numerous letters from the frontier in Pennsylvania Archives, First Series, vols. viii. and xii. The latter volume contains Brodhead's Letter Book.
2 Albach's Western Annals, p. 311; Magazine of American History, vol. iii.

Great was the destruction of animals and birds in the forest. The snow was so deep that they could not get food, and when the spring came the hunters found only the dead bodies of deer, turkeys and smaller game. The Indians suffered sorely in their woodland villages. Especially was the destitution great among the Senecas, whose corn and vegetables had been destroyed by Sullivan and Brodhead. In Western New York scores of Senecas died of starvation and cold. Increased hatred of the Americans was the result, and revenge is very sweet to the Indian.[3]

This hard winter so weakened and distressed the Senecas that when spring came they could not renew their raids on Westmoreland county. Their hunters found it necessary to look after game, and this was exceedingly scarce and poor. The settlers of Westmoreland thus enjoyed an unusual opportunity to plant their fields and gardens, but this immunity was not granted to the inhabitants of the region between the Monongahela and Ohio rivers, under the jurisdiction of Virginia.

That part of the frontier was troubled by the Indians of the Ohio tribes, either Shawnees from the Scioto, or Wyandots and Muncys from the Sandusky. These tribes had not been without plentiful stores of corn, and had passed a comfortable winter. They were supplied with guns, ammunition and clothing by the British at Detroit and were ready to take the warpath as soon as the snow began to melt. The Shawnees were occupied with the growing and aggressive settlements of Kentucky. The bold warriors of the Wyandot or Huron nation fell upon the settlements on the Ohio river and its tributaries.

On a Sunday morning, March 12, 1780, a party of five men and six children were at a sugar camp on Raccoon creek, in the southern end of what is now Beaver county. They had probably been at the camp all night, boiling the maple syrup. At dawn a party of Wyandots, having crept up cautiously, shot and tomahawked the five men and carried away the children, three boys and three girls. This

---

[3] Magazine of American History, vol. iii., p. 667.

was the first blow of the opening season.⁴ Others followed, along the Ohio border. In some instances the Indians only stole horses or slaughtered cattle and hogs.

Toward the end of March a band of Muncy warriors, led by Washnash, a notorious bandit, attacked and captured a flatboat going down the Ohio river to Kentucky. Three men were killed and 21 men, women and children were captured.⁵ On April 27 Colonel Brodhead wrote to the president of Pennsylvania: "Between 40 and 50 men, women and children have been killed or taken from what are now called the counties of Yohogania, Monongalia and Ohio, but no damage is yet done in Westmoreland."⁶

Brodhead wrote to the militia officers of the frontier counties to get men ready to aid him in an expedition against the Ohio Indians, but when he began to make his preparations he found that he could not gather enough provisions for a week ahead.⁷ Throughout the war the western garrisons were hampered by lack of commissary supplies. The cost of carrying stores over the mountain roads was great, frequently exceeding the original cost of the articles. The pack trains were delayed by many circumstances. There were frequent robberies, sometimes by the men in charge of the transportation. Money was scarce, officials were incompetent, and administration lacked system. A great part of the expense and labor was wasted on whisky, which was considered a necessary feature of the commissary supply.

Westmoreland county raised a few militiamen, who reoccupied posts along the Allegheny and Kiskiminetas rivers. The state was so poor and so slow that for two months the expense was paid by a subscription among the principal settlers. The governing authorities at Philadelphia were, in fact, losing faith in the militia, and even in regulars, as a means of frontier protection. In spite of these soldiers, permanent and temporary, the Indians made their raids

---

4 Pennsylvania Archives, vol. viii., pp. 140, 152, 159.
5 Pennsylvania Archives, vol. viii., p. 159.
6 Pennsylvania Archives, vol. viii., p. 210.
7 Pennsylvania Archives, vol. viii., pp. 249, 518; Ft. Pitt, pp. 235, 236.

and their slaughters year after year, with trifling losses to themselves. The Supreme Executive Council decided to try another method, and rewards were offered for Indian and tory prisoners and scalps, $1,500 for a male prisoner and $1,000 for a male scalp. It was hoped that this would stimulate the young men of the frontier to active operations.[8]

Early in May, Brodhead sent Godfrey Lanctot, a Frenchman who spoke several Indian languages, to visit the Ohio tribes and endeavor to persuade them into peace, but his efforts were fruitless. The Shawnees, Wyandots and Muncys would not listen to him.[9]

In May the Senecas, having somewhat recovered from the blow inflicted upon them, came down the Allegheny again in small bands and did considerable damage in Westmoreland. They killed and captured five persons near Ligonier, burned Laughlin's mill, killed two men on Bushy run and killed two on Braddock's old road near Turtle creek.[10] The settlers left their scattered homes and gathered in the stockade forts and blockhouses, but the danger was soon over. The season was a very dry one, and the Allegheny river became so low that even the Indian canoes could not navigate it. The incursions from the north thereupon ceased.

Danger still threatened from the west and Brodhead received a report that an army of British and Indians was assembling on the Sandusky river, in preparation for an attack in force on Fort Pitt. He directed Lieutenant Brady to take a few chosen men, go to Sandusky and find out what was going on there. With five white companions and two Delawares, all dressed and painted like Indians, Brady set out late in May. His journey was a long, arduous and dangerous one. As they approached the Wyandot country the scouts traveled only by night, hiding in the thickest woods by day. One of the Delawares lost heart and returned to Fort Pitt.

---

8 Pennsylvania Archives, vol. viii., pp. 217, 218, 283.
9 Pennsylvania Archives, vol. viii., pp. 301, 551.
10 Pennsylvania Archives, vol. viii., pp. 246, 282.

Brady and his men drew near the Wyandot capital, near Upper Sandusky, and at night the lieutenant and one Delaware companion waded to a wooded island, directly opposite the Indian town. There they lay in a thicket all the next day, watching the savages enjoying a horse race near the river bank. The town was overcrowded with warriors, and their festivities indicated preparations for the warpath.

At nightfall Brady and his Indian withdrew, rejoined their waiting companions and hurried away toward Fort Pitt. About two miles from Sandusky they surprised and captured two young squaws at an Indian camp, and took them along, thinking they might give valuable information. At the end of six days one of the squaws escaped. The food carried by the scouts was exhausted, and for a week they lived on berries. Game was exceedingly scarce. Brady shot an otter, but its flesh was so rank that even these hungry men could not eat it.

Near the old Indian town of Kuskuskee, at the junction of the Mahoning and Shenango rivers, when their powder was reduced to only two charges, Brady saw a deer and was able to approach within certain shooting distance of it. He pulled the trigger, but his gun flashed in the pan. He quickly stirred up the priming, and was preparing again to fire, when he heard human voices, the voices of Indians. Keeping well concealed, he saw, coming along a trail through the forest, an Indian captain riding a gray horse, followed by six warriors afoot. Riding behind the captain was a captive woman, and the Indian held the woman's child in his arms.

Brady knew the woman as Mrs. Jennie Stoops, of the Chartiers creek settlement, and he did not hesitate for an instant. As the Indian leader came opposite him he took careful aim and shot him through the head. The savage fell dead from his horse, dragging the woman and child with him. Brady dashed forward, shouting for his men to come on. The surprised warriors fired a shot or two and fled into the woods. Brady lifted the woman. She did not know him for a white man. "I am Sam Brady," he said;

"follow me." Then he seized the child and hurried away, followed by the woman. He found his men, cowering in the thickets. In their fear and excitement, they had allowed the other Wyandot squaw to escape.

After going a few miles along the trail toward Fort McIntosh, the scouts met a band of settlers from the Chartiers valley, pursuing the marauders. Mrs. Stoops and her infant were restored unharmed to the husband and father. Brady then returned with a party to the scene of the adventure, where he found and scalped the Wyandot captain. He returned to Fort Pitt, after an absence of 32 days. The one Delaware who had run away had reported that the whole party had been killed or captured, and so great was the joy of the garrison over Brady's return that he was greeted with volley after volley of musketry as he crossed the river and entered the fort. Colonel Brodhead recommended Brady's promotion, and on July 25 the Supreme Executive Council made him a captain, dating his commission and pay from the preceding September.[11]

---

[11] Pennsylvania Archives, vol. viii., pp. 378, 769; Colonial Records, vol. xii., p. 436; Winning of the West, vol. iii., p. 57; Hist. Coll. of Pa., p. 105.

CHAPTER XVII.

THE SUMMER OF THE BIG HARVEST.

During the summer of 1780 the soldiers in Fort Pitt were hungry in the midst of plenty. It was a strange situation. The wheat harvest was bounteous, and afterward the corn came very heavy. It has often been noted that the land yields well when the winter has been hard. Some say that the deep frost, stirring and loosening the soil, makes the earth richer. The gardens are more productive in vegetables, but severe cold is hard on the fruit trees.

After the Westmoreland farmers had cut and threshed their wheat, beating it out with the flail, the streams were so dry that no mills could run, and so there was no flour for Colonel Brodhead to buy.[1] But this was not the only reason he did not get food for his garrison. His men suffered for fresh meat, and the farmers would not sell their cattle. To be honest with them, they did not have many cattle to sell. The Indian raids of the preceding three years had been destructive to the live stock. A dozen Indians would kill a great many domestic animals. They not only shot the animals for their own eating, but slaughtered them out of pure wantonness and to deprive the white men of food.

The settlers were reluctant to part with their cattle, because Colonel Brodhead had no good money to pay for them. He could offer nothing but due bills, to be redeemed by the government in its continental currency. This cur-

---
1 Archives, vol. viii., pp. 487, 514; vol. xii., p. 252.

rency the western farmers did not desire, because it was so depreciated that $40 of it were equal to but $1 of the money of the state of Pennsylvania. Moreover, to get these due bills redeemed it was necessary to carry them or send them all the way to Philadelphia. The colonel might have been more successful with state money, but of that he did not have much. It maintained its credit largely because it was scarce. Even the state money, in this year of 1780, was not in full favor west of the Alleghany Mountains.[2]

The pioneers conceived that they had been neglected by the state, and a spirit of discontent and sedition was widely prevalent on the western border. This had been stimulated by the territorial dispute between Pennsylvania and Virginia, which involved the entire Monongahela valley region. Many of the pioneers favored the erection of a new state, to be composed of the over-mountain lands of Pennsylvania and Virginia, believing that they would receive better treatment from a state capital in the Ohio valley, than from the distant governments at Philadelphia and Richmond. The agitation for a new state was vigorous during this summer, and the settlers who favored it looked with hostility upon the garrison of regular soldiers kept at Fort Pitt. The removal of that garrison by starvation would not have been considered by the pioneers as a calamity.[3]

Colonel Brodhead was driven to many expedients to get food. On August 18, 1780, he wrote to the president of Pennsylvania: "The troops have been without bread for several days and begin to murmur; but I expect to get a little grain chopped in a bad horse mill near this place, and, if possible, prevent a mutiny until a further supply can be procured. I hear the pack horse men have left the service, so that not a shilling have we to purchase with." At this time the lack of food had compelled the evacuation of Forts Armstrong and Crawford on the Allegheny river.[4]

---

2 Archives, vol. viii., p. 515.
3 Archives, vol. vii., pp. 280, 713.
4 Archives, vol. vii., p. 513.

The Pennsylvania authorities gave up the plan of carrying supplies to Fort Pitt on horses from the eastern part of the state, and made effort to furnish the garrison from the county of Westmoreland. For this work they appointed William Amberson, one of the earliest settlers of Pittsburg, as commissary, and directed him to furnish flour, corn and whisky to Colonel Brodhead. Amberson seems to have been but partially successful in getting supplies, for on September 5 Colonel Brodhead wrote: "The troops have alternately been destitute of bread and meat. At present I am not possessed of two days' allowance, and I have a dull prospect as to further supplies. I have been compelled to hire a few horses to send to the mills below. . . . Unless something is speedily done, these posts, which are of the utmost importance, must be evacuated, and the country will, of course, be deserted, or, as some have hinted, join the enemy."[5]

About a week after this letter was written, the entire garrison of Fort Pitt paraded one morning before the house of Colonel Brodhead, ragged and gaunt, led by their sergeants. When the commander asked the cause of the demonstration, the sergeants replied that the men had been without bread for five days and were hungry.

Colonel Brodhead was able to tell them only that every effort was making to get food for them, and that, during the period of scarcity, their officers were suffering equally with the rank and file. The men were well behaved and quietly returned to their barracks. A few days afterward a few horse loads of flour and some live cattle arrived from Cumberland county, but this supply did not last long.[6]

During this time the surrounding country was being ravaged by the Indians, and a starving garrison could offer no protection. On August 11 a party of Wyandot Indians killed ten men near the site of Morgantown, W. Va.[7] On September 4 two settlers were killed near Robinson's

---

5 Archives, vol. viii., p. 536.
6 Archives, vol. viii., p. 558.
7 Archives, vol. viii., p. 513.

run, now in Allegheny county. The same day two men going down the Ohio river in a canoe to Wheeling were fired upon from the bank, and one of them was wounded.[8] About the middle of September the Wyandots fell upon the settlements on Ten Mile creek and killed and carried away seven persons.[9] Brodhead was fretting over his compulsory inaction. Time and again he summoned the militia to rally for a raid into the Wyandot land and each time he was baffled by the lack of supplies.

At length, in September, Colonel Brodhead, driven to desperation, determined to take extreme measures to get food for his hungry soldiers. He had received from the continental authorities permission to take supplies by force from the inhabitants, in case of dire need, and to this resort he was now driven. He chose Captain Samuel Brady to do this work, with a detachment from his company.[10]

Brady was instructed to attempt to buy cattle and sheep only from those who had them to spare, and, if the farmers would not sell, he was then to take the animals by force. He was not to molest the poor or those who had suffered from the Indians. All cattle and sheep siezed were to be appraised and Brady was to give a receipt for them, so that the owners might have a chance some time to recover from the United States government. Brady went into the country along Chartiers creek and on the western side of the Monongahela river, while Lieutenant Uriah Springer headed another party east of the Monongahela.

News of Brady's mission seems to have spread rapidly before him. Many of the larger herds of cattle were driven into secluded forest recesses. In few places did the soldiers find stock to be spared, within the terms of their instructions. They did get some and sent them back to the fort, but they were not sufficient for the daily wants of the garrison. There was show of strong resistance to the impressing squad. In some places Brady was threatened with writs

---

8 Archives, vol. viii., p. 536.
9 Archives, vol. viii., p. 559.
10 Crumrine's History of Washington County, p. 89; Pennsylvania Archives, vol. viii., pp. 565, 589; vol. xii., pp. 276, 278.

of trespass. Crowds of angry and armed settlers gathered and made show of forcible resistance. Brady's instructions commanded him not to provoke violence, without extreme cause, but the signs began to multiply that the country was preparing to rise against him. It was probably the most unpleasant task he was ever called upon to perform. He was himself a farmer, and could not fail to sympathize with these badgered and distressed pioneers. For two months he and Springer were kept in the field before the persistent Brodhead ordered their withdrawal.

Early in October, when Brodhead had hope that Brady would bring enough beef and mutton to supply an expedition into the Wyandot country, he sent out another appeal to the lieutenants of the adjacent counties to raise volunteers and join him at Fort Pitt. This appeal was a total failure. Colonel Beelor, of Yohogania county, replied that he could not get volunteers. The only way he could help Brodhead was to draft men, and this he feared to attempt, as he did not know whether to proceed under the law of Pennsylvania or Virginia. It was just about this time that the governments of the two states were coming to an agreement on the boundary line, and reports had reached the frontier that all the disputed territory would fall within the bounds of Pennsylvania. These reports caused legal chaos in what is now Southwestern Pennsylvania. The laws of Virginia lost their binding effect and the executive and judicial machinery of Pennsylvania had not yet been extended over the region so long in contention. Thus it was that Beelor found himself powerless to act, and in signing his name to his letter to Brodhead he rather pathetically added, "Without law to protect me."[11]

The reply of Colonel William McCleery, of Monongalia county, is interesting as revealing the stubborn self-reliance of the Scotch-Irish settlers on the upper Monongahela and Cheat rivers. The militia officers of that county met and decided that they could not spare any men to assist the

---

[11] Pennsylvania Archives, vol. viii., pp. 352, 583, 589; vol. x., pp. 171, 173; Craig's History of Pittsburg, p. 124.

regulars in an expedition to the northwest. Colonel McCleery wrote:

"From his (Brodhead's) never having it in his power, for want, as we conceive, of the necessary supplies to put his schemes in execution, during the whole course of last summer and fall, and our unhappy people daily falling an easy prey to the enemy, obliges them to throw off all dependence on any natural aid on this side of the mountains this fall, but that of themselves, for their relief, and therefore they mean to embody and and take the most plausible methods for their defense, and under the circumstances they think their number is already too small without any division."[12]

The Delaware chiefs, still true to their alliance with the Americans, came to Fort Pitt with a large band of warriors, to take part in the Wyandot campaign. Their chagrin was keen when Brodhead told them of his poverty and want of food, and that they could not have the opportunity of going with him on a war raid.

While these Indians, with their women and children, were encamped near the fort, a large party of settlers from Hannastown, led by militia officers, marched to Fort Pitt for the purpose of attacking the friendly savages. A majority of the pioneers of that day did not distinguish between one redskin and another. All were "pizen varmints," and equally deserving of death. Colonel Brodhead was forewarned and threw a heavy guard of regulars around the Indian camp. The design of the Westmorelanders was frustrated, and they were forced to return with bloodless hands to Hannastown. The same spirit which animated them led the men of Washington county, 16 months afterward, to murder the Christianized Delawares at Gnadenhuetten.[13]

It was fortunate for Brodhead that he was able to protect these Indians, for he found use for them after the failure of Brady's cattle impressment. He made arrangement for

---
12 Pennsylvania Archives, vol. viii., p. 584.
13 Pennsylvania Archives, vol. viii., p. 596.

a considerable body of them, as well as some of the best hunters among his soldiers, to go to the Great Kanawha valley, to spend the winter there hunting buffaloes and to bring the meat to Fort Pitt as soon as the river should open in the spring.[14] It was to such measures that he was driven to feed his soldiers. During the winter, however, some meat and flour were procured from the eastern counties, and the garrison managed to live without leaving any record of a death from actual starvation. The number of the garrison during the winter of 1780-81 was about 300.

---

14 Olden Time, vol. ii., pp. 377, 378.

CHAPTER XVIII.

THE DERRY SETTLEMENT.

The afflictions and daring deeds of the pioneers of the Derry settlement during the Revolution will illustrate the experiences of other districts in the Westmoreland country. Derry was a long, triangular territory near the northern border of the county, bounded on the east by Chestnut Ridge, on the north by Conemaugh river, and on the southwest by Loyalhanna creek. Its first settlers were from the Cumberland Valley, and were either natives of Derry, in Ireland, or their immediate descendants. The circumstances under which these pioneers went to the border show that they were bold and self-reliant. The time was a year or two prior to the purchase of the land from the Indians, and the settlers were trespassers. Yet they fearlessly penetrated the forest, built their cabins and hewed out their clearings, taking their chances of withstanding the savages on the one hand and the colonial authorities on the other. When the land office opened, in the spring of 1769, most of these Derry "squatters" were successful in obtaining warrants for their holdings.

The leaders in this Derry settlement were Robert Barr, James Wilson, John Pomeroy, William Guthrie, John Shields, Samuel Craig and Richard Wallace. A few of their compatriots, among them Charles Campbell and George Findley, ventured to settle north of the Conemaugh river, in the valley of Blacklick creek, where they were in the most exposed situation in all the border region.

The cabins of the Derry men were of logs, and, being furnished with loop-holes for rifles, were capable of stout defense against the Indians. Richard Wallace built on a hill near the Conemaugh, about a mile and a half south of the site of Blairsville. He erected a grist mill which ground the grain of the entire settlement. When Dunmore's war began, in the spring of 1774, he constructed a strong stockade around his house, which afforded a refuge for the neighborhood. This stockade became known as Fort Wallace.

About five and a half miles to the southwest, on a tributary of the Loyalhanna, settled Robert Barr and his sons, and when the Revolution began a stockade was constructed there, known as Fort Barr. A mile farther south, immediately overlooking the Loyalhanna, was the log house of John Shields, and it also was surrounded by a stockade. These three stockades were the strong places of the Derry settlement, frequently assailed but never overcome by the savages. Robert Barr's two sons-in-law, James Wilson and John Pomeroy, dwelt in isolated clearings between Fort Barr and Fort Wallace.

The official records of Pennsylvania contain only occasional references to the perils of the Derry settlement during the Revolution. Details of the adventures of the pioneers have been preserved in family traditions, and some of these have been collected in print. These traditions are far from trustworthy, save as corroborated or corrected by contemporary records. Two events are sometimes mingled into one, circumstances are distorted or exaggerated, and dates are often far out of the way. The men who cleared the woods and fought the savages were either unlettered or too busy with deeds to find time for writing. The human memory is very fallible, and tradition is a fragile support for the historian; yet it serves to give life and color to the dull statements of official reports.

It was in harvest time of 1777 that the Indians first raided the northern border of Westmoreland. North of the Kiskiminetas a few men were killed or captured, and the Blacklick settlers fled away to Fort Wallace with their wives and cattle. Among the fugitives was Randall Laughlin, whose horses escaped from the pasture at Fort Wallace and returned to the Blacklick farm. Laughlin determined to venture back after them, and was accompanied by four of his neighbors, Charles Campbell, a major of the militia; two brothers Gibson, and a man of the name of Dixon. In safety they reached Laughlin's cabin, and while resting there on Sept. 25, they were surprised and surrounded by a band of savages, probably Wyandots, led by a Frenchman. On the promise that their lives would be spared, the settlers surrendered. They were permitted to write a note, describing their capture, and to tack it on the cabin door. Then they were hurried away, through the wilderness, to Detroit. Rangers who went in search of the missing men, found the note on the door and within the cabin four printed proclamations, from Governor Hamilton, of Detroit, offering reward to all who would desert the American cause. Along the Blacklick valley the rangers discovered the scalped bodies of four settlers, whose lives had been the forfeit of their temerity.[1]

Major Campbell and his companions were taken to Quebec, where they were liberated on exchange in the fall of 1778. Dixon and one of the Gibsons died on shipboard during the voyage to Boston, but the three others returned to the Westmoreland frontier, where Campbell subsequently attained high position.

Several small parties of savages prowled through the Derry settlement during the autumn of 1777, stealing and killing live stock and burning deserted cabins. The settlers kept close in the three forts and suffered little personal injury. On November 1 Lieutenant Samuel Craig, who lived near Shields's fort, was riding toward Ligonier for salt, when he was waylaid and killed or captured at the western base of Chestnut Ridge. Rangers found his beautiful mare

---

[1] Pennsylvania Archives, vol. v., p. 741; Caldwell's History of Indiana County, p. 140; Thomas Galbraith's Journal, in Frontier Forts, vol. ii., p. 237.

lying dead near the trail, with eight bullets in her, but not the slightest trace of the rider was ever discovered.[2]

Three days after the taking of Craig, the Indians attacked Fort Wallace. The savages opened fire from the edge of the woods on one side of the fort, while on the other side a white man appeared, wading in the shallow water up the tail race of the mill and waving a red flag. His action was a mystery to the defenders of the stockade, but their curiosity did not restrain their triggers. As the flag bearer approached the palisade, he received a volley and fell dead with seven bullets in his body. In a bag suspended from a cord around his neck were found two proclamations like those left in Randall Laughlin's cabin on the Blacklick. He was one of Hamilton's emissaries from Detroit, and when he fell his savage followers glided away into the woods.[3]

The Indians did not leave the settlement. Major James Wilson, working about his farm, heard the firing of guns at the cabin of a neighbor. Wilson got his rifle and went to investigate. He found his neighbor's body, the head being severed and lying near. Wilson then hurried his wife and children to Fort Barr, and a party of the borderers, led by Robert Barr, was soon gathered to pursue the marauders. This party included two of the most experienced Indian trailers on the frontier, Major James Smith and Captain John Hinkston. The Indians were followed across the Kiskiminetas toward the Allegheny river, and were overtaken near Kittanning. A sharp conflict ensued, five of the savages were killed and the others were dispersed. The dead savages were scalped, and the ghastly trophies were sent to Philadelphia for reward.[4]

In the spring of 1778 the Indians came down again, across the Kiskiminetas and the Conemaugh. On April 28 a score of rangers, under the command of Captain Hopkins, who had gone out from Fort Wallace, were surprised

---

2 Galbraith's Journal, Frontier Forts, vol. ii., pp. 244, 287.
3 Frontier Forts, vol. ii., p. 244.
4 Greensburg Herald, November 23, 1870; Pennsylvania Archives, vol. vi., p. 69.

by a superior force of savages in the forest and were defeated after a hard fight. Nine of the rangers were slain and their bodies left behind; Captain Hopkins was slightly wounded, and four of the Indians fell.[5]

This is probably the combat in which Ebenezer Finley took part, described in Dr. Joseph Smith's "Old Redstone."[6] Ebenezer was the son of the celebrated pioneer preacher, Rev. James Finley, and, according to the story related of him, was serving a tour at Fort Wallace as a member of a small militia company from the Monongahela valley. A horseman dashed into the fort, with an alarm that Indians were in the vicinity, that he had left two men and a woman coming in through the woods afoot, and that they must be overtaken if not rapidly succored. Eighteen or twenty militiamen sallied forth, and, at a distance of about a mile and a half from the fort, fell into an Indian ambush. After the first exchange of shots, the militiamen retreated, and a running fight took place nearly to the gate of the fort. Many of the white men "were shot down or tomahawked." Finley fell behind while trying to prime his gun, and was in imminent danger of being overtaken. Putting forth extra effort, he succeeded in passing a comrade by striking the other man on the shoulder with his elbow, and a moment later this comrade was felled with a tomahawk. Thus young Finley saved himself by sacrificing the life of another, and the pious author would have it that Finley escaped by the interposition of Providence. Rev. James Finley was in Philadelphia at the time, and at the very hour of the ambuscade was affected by a strong impression that his son was in danger. He betook himself to intense prayer, and after a short period was relieved by a feeling that the danger had passsed. It was not until several weeks later that he learned the nature of his son's peril and the manner of his escape.

Certain family traditions of the Derry settlement relate

---

5 Pennsylvania Archives, vol. vi., pp. 469, 495.
6 Old Redstone, or Historical Sketches of Western Presbyterianism, Philadelphia, 1854, p. 284.

THE DERRY SETTLEMENT.

to another bitter combat with the savages in the immediate neighborhood of Fort Wallace, at an uncertain period during the Revolution. This affair may have taken place during the summer of 1778, for it is known that desperate inroads were made by the Indians at that time into the northern precincts of Westmoreland.[7] The story goes that signs of Indians were seen near Fort Barr, and the settlers throughout the southern part of Derry took refuge there. They were preparing to withstand an attack, when brisk firing was heard in the direction of Fort Wallace. Major James Wilson, at the head of about forty men, promptly set out from Barr's to the relief of the other post. They arrived within sight of Fort Wallace, which they found heavily besieged, but as soon as Wilson's company appeared, the savages turned upon it and assailed it in overwhelming force. The principal conflict took place on a bridge over a deep gully, about 500 yards from the fort. Several Indians were there slain and others were thrown over the bridge; but Wilson's party was forced to retreat and fought desperately all the way back to Fort Barr. During this retreat two of Robert Barr's sons, Alexander and Robert, were killed, but their bodies were saved from the scalping knife. All others gained the stockade in safety, and the Indians soon afterward disappeared from the settlement.[8]

No record has been found of further Indian attacks on the Derry district until the spring of 1781. On the first day of April, while Colonel John Pomeroy and at least three hired men were at work in a field, they were fired upon by Indians and one of the men was killed. Pomeroy fled to his cabin, while the two hired men ran for Fort Barr, about a mile away. Only one of them reached the fort, where he related what had occurred. Very few men were in the fort, but James Wilson and James Barr mounted horses and rode away to Pomeroy's assistance. From a hilltop near

---

7 Fort Pitt, pp. 232, 238.

8 Greensburg Herald, November 23, 1870; Frontier Forts, vol. ii., p. 347.

the house they saw several Indians skulking about Pomeroy's barn, but no sound came from the cabin. Wilson called out, "Pomeroy, are you alive?" From the cabin came the lusty response, "Yes; come on and we'll kill all the rascals yet." Wilson and Barr left their horses, made a dash for the dwelling and entered it unharmed. There they found that the owner and his wife Hannah had been making a gallant defense for nearly three hours. They had hidden their children under the heavy oak floor and had betaken themselves to the loft, from whose port holes Pomeroy had been firing. He had two good rifles, and, while he was handling one, Hannah loaded the other, taking, meanwhile, frequent liberal pinches of snuff.

Upon the arrival of Wilson and Barr, the Indians, who were few in number, ran to the woods. The children were drawn from their hiding place and Pomeroy's family was conducted, without molestation, to Fort Barr.[9] On the following day Colonel Archibald Lochry, the county lieutenant, arrived in the settlement with a company of militia and visited Pomeroy's farm. The dwelling had been broken open by the Indians, and nearly all the contents carried away. In the field the body of the scalped laborer was found and buried. A second hired man, who had fled, was never found.[10]

---

9 Greensburg Herald, November 23, 1870.
10 Pennsylvania Archives, First Series, vol. ix., p. 51.

CHAPTER XIX.

THE DESTRUCTION OF COSHOCTON.

Colonel Brodhead was never able to execute his design to lead a force against the Wyandot or the Shawnee towns in Ohio. He had expected to get help, for such an expedition, from the Delaware warriors at Coshocton, but in the spring of 1781 a change in the situation impelled him to strike the Delawares themselves. Until the beginning of that year the Delawares took no part, as a tribe, in the war against the frontier. The alliance with the United States, made by their three principal chiefs in the autumn of 1778, was outwardly observed for more than two years. The death of White Eyes had been followed by the election of Killbuck, a famous medicine man and warrior, to the office of chief sachem, and he proved himself to be an unswerving friend to the Americans. It was soon developed, however, that he represented a minority of his tribe. His influence was sufficient merely to delay the union of the Delawares with the other hostile nations.

Brodhead had nothing to give to the Indians; British agents from Detroit gave not only promises but presents. Envoys from the Senecas, the Wyandots, the Miamis and tribes farther to the west visited the Delaware towns often, threatening and persuading and using all savage arts to draw the chiefs and warriors into the league against the Americans. Raiding parties going homeward from the frontier flaunted their trophies in the Delaware villages and stirred the envy and ambition of the young bucks. The

Indian inclines to war rather than to peace. Captain Pipe became the leader of the war party and soon controlled the tribal council.

In February, 1781, during the absence of Killbuck at Fort Pitt, the council at Coshocton yielded to the pressure, voted to join the hostile league and permitted bands of warriors to go out against the Pennsylvania and Virginia border.

Killbuck feared to return to Coshocton, for threats had been boldly uttered against his life. He made his residence with the Moravians or United Brethren and their converted Indians at Salem, on the western bank of the Tuscarawas river, 14 miles below New Philadelphia. He even professed conversion to Christianity, was baptized and received a Christian name, William Henry, in honor of a distinguished citizen of Lancaster, Pa. Thereafter the Indian sachem, who held a commission from the United States Congress, was proud to call himself "Colonel Henry." He drew to Salem with him his own family, the family of White Eyes and a few other Delawares, including the war captains Big Cat and Nanowland. From Salem Chief Killbuck wrote, by the hand of the Missionary Heckewelder, a long letter to Colonel Brodhead, informing him of the hostile acts of the council at Coshocton.[1]

This letter was accompanied by one from Heckewelder and both were carried to Fort Pitt by John Montour. Heckewelder suggested an expedition against Coshocton, adding: "I trust that your honor will do all that lies in your power to prevent mislisting anybody belonging to our towns; and you may depend, sir, that in case any of your men should have occasion to come by any of our towns, they would meet with much kindness from our people."

Brodhead determined to attack Coshocton and punish the Delawares for their perfidy. Vigorous exertions by the Pennsylvania government had given him a supply of provisions, but his force of regulars at Fort Pitt had been reduced, from various causes, to about 200 men. To the

---

[1] Pennsylvania Archives, First Series, vol. viii., pp. 769-771.

THE DESTRUCTION OF COSHOCTON.

officers of the border counties he sent a call for militia assistance, but this call was fruitless.[2] By the help of Colonel David Shepherd, of Wheeling, who was county lieutenant of Ohio county, Pa., Brodhead was able to secure a body of excellent volunteers. There were 134 of them, members of the Virginia militia, arranged in four companies, under Captains John Ogle, Benjamin Royce, Jacob Lefler and William Crawford.[3] These men were hardy young farmers and hunters from the settlements in Washington county and along the left bank of the Ohio. Most of them rode their own horses and joined in the raid under Colonel Shepherd's command.

Fort Henry, the stockade at Wheeling, was the place of assembly, and to that place Brodhead and his soldiers went down in boats during the first week in April. On Tuesday, April 10, the little army, about 300 strong, was ferried over the Ohio river and took the Indian trail for the Muskingum river. John Montour, Nanowland and three other Delaware braves went with the Americans to fight their own tribesmen.

It was very desirable that the expedition should move rapidly, so that it might take the Indian village by surprise; yet it was ten days before Brodhead's force appeared before Coshocton. The weather was bad, a great deal of rain fell and progress was difficult. The commander paused awhile, when he neared the Tuscarawas, for a conference with Rev. John Heckewelder, the missionary among the Delawares. A messenger sent ahead had summoned the Moravian minister from his Huts of Grace on the Tuscarawas river, and he met Brodhead on the trail. Brodhead wished to know if any of the Christian Indians were in the hostile towns. Heckewelder said there was none. Brodhead wished the Moravians to prepare some corn and cattle for the soldiers against their return march. Heckewelder departed to see that it was done. Back to Gnadenhuetten and Salem the missionary bore the news that the Americans were in the

---
2 Pennsylvania Archives, First Series, vol. ix., pp. 51, 52.
3 Washington-Irvine Correspondence, p. 52.

Indian country, and Chief Killbuck and his few warriors put on their paint and went forth to strike a blow for the American cause. Thus the forces of savagery were divided against themselves.

From the Ohio river to the forking of the Muskingum was hardly 70 miles, and that this required ten days showed how bad the weather and the way must have been. Yet in spite of this slow toil, the Delawares were really taken by surprise. They had no expectation of such prompt action by the American commander and kept no scouts abroad in the rainy weather. Perhaps most important of all, some of their chief men were at Detroit, attending a great council of all the tribes of the northwest, with DePeyster, the British governor. This embassy probably included the Pipe, who had become chief sachem of the tribe in place of Killbuck, deposed, and the famous war chief called the Beloved. Buckongahelas or He-Who-Fulfils, the next chief in authority, was probably away with a raiding band, and thus Coshocton was without a head and unprepared even for defensive action.

On Friday, April 20, in the morning, while the rain was pouring, the American advance guard came upon three Indians in the woods, not more than a mile from Coshocton. One of the savages was captured, but the two others, of whom one was wounded, escaped to the town and gave the first alarm. The captured Indian said there were not many warriors at home, that a band of 40 had just returned from a raid on the settlements, with scalps and prisoners, but had crossed to the farther side of the river, a few miles above the town, to enjoy a drunken revel.

Brodhead hurried forward and dashed into the Delaware capital. But 15 warriors were there, who made as brave a resistance as they could, but every one of them was either shot down or tomahawked to death in the resistless rush of the Americans. The mounted volunteers were naturally first into the town and they neither accepted surrender by an Indian buck nor suffered any of the wounded to linger long in agony. No harm was done to the old men, women or children, of whom more than a score were captured. These were removed, under guard, to a place outside the town, and the log cabins composing Coshocton were then given to the flames.

The colonel said, in his official report, that his men took "great quantities of peltry and other stores" and destroyed about 40 head of cattle. Doubtless there was a great feast on beef when the work of killing and burning was over, for the tired troops were not so well provisioned that they would let fresh meat go to waste.

Brodhead desired to cross the river and attack the drunken war party, but the stream was swollen to the tops of its banks and the Indians had all their canoes on the farther side. It was the high water which had prevented the escape of all the inhabitants of Coshocton. The commander then proposed to send a detail to the Moravian towns, up the Tuscarawas, to procure boats, but against this the volunteers protested. They said they had done enough, had suffered sorely from the weather, had almost worn out their horses and proposed to return home. As they were in no way subjected to military discipline. Colonel Brodhead could not help himself.

On the return journey, the Americans followed the Tuscarawas to Newcomer's Town, where they found about 30 friendly Delawares who had withdrawn from Coshocton, when war was voted. Colonel Brodhead says: "The troops experienced great kindness from the Moravian Indians and those at Newcomer's Town and obtained a sufficient supply of meat and corn to subsist the men and horses to the Ohio river."

If Brodhead was unable to strike the hostile band on the farther side of the river, that work was done by Chief Killbuck and his adherents. While the Americans rested at Newcomer's Town, Killbuck appeared in the camp and threw at the colonel's feet the fresh scalp of "one of the greatest villains" among the hostiles.

The expedition returned to Wheeling about the beginning of May, where the furs and other captured goods were sold at vendue, bringing the astonishing sum of 80,000 pounds. The furs were the product of a winter's hunting.[4]

Quite a different story of this expedition is to be found in the old histories. Its author was Rev. Joseph Doddridge, of Washington county, who gave it forth in his once popular "Notes on the Settlements and Indian Wars, etc." His story was copied almost word for word in Craig's "History of Pittsburg," and is adhered to in Howe's "Historical Collections of Ohio," revised as recently as 1890.[5]

Doddridge said that the raid took place in the summer of 1780, which was nearly a year out of the way, and that the force consisted of about 800 regulars and "militia." No militia responded as an organization to Brodhead's call, and that officer, in his report, was careful to refer to the Virginians who aided him as "volunteers." The whole force, said Brodhead, was "about 300 men."

Doddridge said: "The whole number of the Indians in the village . . . were made prisoners without firing a single shot. . . . A little after dark a council of war was held to determine on the fate of the warriors in custody. They were doomed to death, and, by order of the commander, they were bound, taken a little distance below the town and dispatched with tomahawks and spears and scalped."

This was a vicious accusation against Colonel Brodhead and is contradictory of the whole history of that strict disciplinarian and high-minded officer. The town was not taken without a shot. Brodhead's report said: "The troops behaved with great spirit, and although there was considerable firing between them and the Indians, I had not a man killed or wounded, and only one horse shot."

But Rev. Mr. Doddridge was only warming to his work. Here is his conclusion of the story: "Brodhead committed the care of the prisoners to the militia. They were about 20 in number. After marching about half a

---

4 For Brodhead's Report, Pennsylvania Archives, First Series, vol. ix., p. 161.
5 Doddridge's Notes, p. 291; Howe's Historical Collections of Ohio, vol. i., p. 480; Western Annals, p. 330.

mile, the men commenced killing them. In a short time they were all dispatched, except a few women and children, who were spared and taken to Fort Pitt, and, after some time, were exchanged for an equal number of their prisoners."

The only truth in this statement consists in the number of the prisoners. It may be said that Colonel Brodhead would not be likely to mention so disgraceful an affair in his report, and that his silence is therefore no evidence that the prisoners were not butchered. But the story is disproved by the testimony of the enemy. A few days after Colonel Brodhead retired, the ruins of Coshocton were visited by twenty Wyandots, who learned from the released prisoners and other survivors the particulars of the American raid. These Wyandots quickly bore the news to Simon Girty, at Upper Sandusky, and he promptly sent a letter to Lieutenant Governor DePeyster at Detroit. Girty had reasons to hate Colonel Brodhead and would have reported that officer's conduct in the worst possible light. Yet Girty wrote that Brodhead had released the prisoners, including four warriors who had satisfied him that they had not engaged in hostilities against the frontier, and had even expressed regret to these Indian men that their tribesmen had been killed during the attack on the Indian town.⁶

Doddridge's book has still thousands of readers. Doubtless, it well describes the conditions of pioneer life in Western Pennsylvania, but as to historical events it is totally unreliable. At the time Brodhead destroyed Coshocton, Joseph Doddridge was about 12 years old, and he did not write his "Notes" until 40 years afterward. His only sources of information were the exaggerated yarns told by ignorant frontiersmen, beside the log cabin fires, into the ears of the wondering boy. Long years afterward he endeavored to recall and set down these stories heard in childhood, and many persons have considered the result history. The official report of Colonel Brodhead, kept among the archives at Harrisburg, was not made public until 1854, and

---

6 The Girtys, p. 128. See also Winsor's Westward Movement, p. 192.

other contemporary records, bearing on the Coshocton campaign, have come to light in later years.

As a result of the Coshocton campaign, the hostile Delawares migrated to the headwaters of the Sandusky and to other places farther westward, while the portion of the tribe adhering to Killbuck and the American moved to Pittsburg and erected their rude cabins on Smoky Island, at the northern side of the junction of the Allegheny and the Monongahela.

CHAPTER XX.

GENERAL CLARK'S DRAFT.

During the spring and summer months of 1781 the Pennsylvania frontier was sorely disturbed by the efforts of General George Rogers Clark to raise troops for an expedition, in the interest of Virginia, against the British post at Detroit. In the summer of 1778 Clark had conquered the Illinois country and the valley of the Wabash for Virginia, and, as it afterward turned out, for the United States. Virginia claimed all that northwestern country by king's charter, but, since king's charters had fallen into disfavor in America, she felt more reliance in a claim based on actual conquest. Clark was ambitious for the enterprise against Detroit and was supported by many of the leading men of the Kentucky and Virginia borders. They saw Detroit as the source of all their afflictions, and were eager for the conquest of that breeding place of savage warfare.

Clark was in Richmond in January, 1781, where the prestige of his exploits easily gained for him the approval and support of the state government. He received a commission as brigadier general and ample funds to buy provisions in the country west of the Alleghany mountains. A small body of Virginia regulars, about 140, was placed at his service and he was empowered to raise and equip volunteers in the border counties.

Agents were sent ahead of Clark into the country between Laurel Hill and the Ohio river and began to buy flour and live cattle.[1] Colonel Brodhead complained to the president of Pennsylvania that the food supply on which he was dependent was to be taken out of the country in the interest of Virginia, and he revealed a jealousy of Clark's enterprise. "I have hitherto been encouraged to flatter myself," he wrote, "that I should, sooner or later, be enabled to reduce that place (Detroit), but it seems the United States cannot furnish either troops or resources for the purpose, but the state of Virginia can."

Brodhead threatened to prevent the sending of any supplies out of the country, but in February he received a letter from General Washington, directing him to give aid to General Clark's undertaking and to detach from his own little force Captain Isaac Craig's field artillery and at least a captain's command of infantry, to assist the Virginia expedition.[2]

General Clark arrived on the Pennsylvania frontier about the beginning of March and made his headquarters at the house of Colonel Crawford, on the Youghiogheny. A part of his time he spent with Colonel Dorsey Pentecost, on Chartiers creek. He instituted vigorous efforts to raise men in the same region where he had found the hardy volunteers for his first raid into the western territory. Then arose a bitter contention throughout all Southwestern Pennsylvania. The frontiersmen seemed to be about equally divided between support and opposition to Clark's plans. It was generally known by this time that all of the Virginia county of Yohogania and much of the counties of Monongalia and Ohio belonged to Pennsylvania, but the boundary line had not been surveyed west of the Monongahela river and the magistrates from Pittsburg southward were all Virginians.

Among the settlers there were many factions. Some would obey no law but that of Pennsylvania, and declared that Clark, as a Virginia officer, had no business in that neighborhood. Others adhered to Virginia until the line

---

[1] Pennsylvania Archives, First Series, vol. viii., p. 767; vol. ix., p. 190.
[2] Pennsylvania Archives, vol. viii., pp. 743, 766, 769.

should be officially surveyed and ardently supported Clark's plans. A few refused to obey any law or acknowledge any jurisdiction, saying they did not know which state was over them. They could not decide such a great dispute, and had enough to do to plant their corn and potatoes and to keep their rifles in good condition for the savages. Some were for a new state of their own, stoutly protesting that the wiseacres at Philadelphia and Richmond never could understand the needs of the over-mountain people. Many of the bolder spirits on the border said they did not care a bad penny whether Clark were a Virginian or a Pennsylvanian; if he could clean out Detroit he would strike a heart blow to the enemy and rescue the border from savage depredations. So they were for him.

Clark's intention was to raise 2,000 men in Southwestern Pennsylvania, float them down the Ohio to the Wabash, ascend that stream as far as possible and march overland to Detroit. When he arrived at Colonel Crawford's he found that the frontiers were being raided by bands of Shawnees from the Scioto, Delawares from the Muskingum and Wyandots from the Sandusky. An expedition against those tribes was more popular among the Pennsylvanians than a campaign against distant Detroit, and therefore Clark made an ostensible change in his plans. He gave it out that he was going against the Ohio savages, for the immediate benefit of the Westmoreland frontier; but his real aim was not altered to conquer Detroit and an additional empire for the Old Dominion.[3]

Brodhead was not deceived, but many Pennsylvania officers were. On March 23 Clark wrote to President Reed, of Pennsylvania, asking his endorsement of the project, for the effect it would have on the frontiersmen who called themselves Pennsylvanians. Clark wrote: "If our resources should not be such as to enable us to remain in the Indian country during the fair season, I am in hopes they will be sufficient to visit the Shawnees, Delawares and San-

---

3 Pennsylvania Archives, vol. ix., pp. 189, 239.

dusky towns. Defeating the enemy and laying those countries waste would give great ease to the frontiers of both states."[4]

President Reed approved of the campaign, but the letters of both Clark and Reed were unreasonably delayed. President Reed wrote, on May 15: "It will give us great satisfaction if the inhabitants of this state cheerfully concur in it, and we authorize you to declare that, so far from giving offense to their government, we shall consider their service with you as highly meritorious."[5] This letter was carried to the frontier by Colonel Christopher Hays, the Westmoreland county member of the Supreme Executive Council. Hays was directed by the council to aid Clark's expedition, but it soon developed that he was opposed to it. Although he arrived in Westmoreland about the beginning of June, the letter which he carried was not delivered to Clark until July 3, when it was too late to do much good.[6]

Hays called a meeting of all the commissioned officers of the Westmoreland militia to arrange a plan for the frontier defense. Doubtless he was confident that he and his friends could control this meeting, but he was disappointed. The officers met on June 18, at the home of Captain John McClelland, on Big Sewickley creek, and, to the chagrin of Colonel Hays, decided by a majority vote to give aid to General Clark. It was resolved to furnish 300 men out of the county militia to join Clark's army, and Colonel Lochry was directed to see that this quota was raised "by volunteers or draft."[7]

This was the first effort made on the Pennsylvania frontier to raise soldiers by draft and it caused a great outcry. The meeting of officers directed Colonel Lochry to consult General Clark respecting the manner of drafting men in Virginia and to agree on a day for a general rendezvous. Lochry met Clark one week later at Crawford's settlement and the rendezvous was ordered for Monday, July

---
4 Pennsylvania Archives, vol. ix., p. 23.
5 Pennsylvania Archives, vol. ix., p. 137.
6 Pennsylvania Archives, vol. ix., pp. 141, 331.
7 Pennsylvania Archives, vol. ix., pp. 239, 247, 369, 559.

16. This day was chosen to enable the farmers to finish their wheat and oats harvesting before taking down their rifles and powder horns.

By act of March 28, 1781, the General Assembly of Pennsylvania created the county of Washington, to comprise all the territory of the state west of the Monongahela river. James Marshel was appointed county lieutenant and he set to work to establish the Pennsylvania jurisdiction in a region where most of the inhabitants were Virginians. The Virginia officers clung to their commissions and were supported by the stronger faction. Such men as Colonel Pentecost, John Canon, Gabriel Cox and Daniel Leet worked hard to muster men for General Clark, while Marshel and his adherents were just as active to defeat the Virginia project. This rivalry, which grew exceedingly bitter, was fatal to Clark's enterprise and unfortunate for the real interests of the frontier. It is probable that Clark, if unitedly supported, would have taken Detroit, overawed the savages and saved the border many years of desolating warfare.[8]

On the day of the rendezvous the attendance at the several designated places was discouragingly small. Clark and his lieutenants immediately proceeded to raise men by draft. Such action was without warrant of law. It gave opportunity for the rougher element among the Virginians to exploit their hatred of their Pennsylvania neighbors. The work of drafting was carried on with many examples of pillage, cruelty and personal violence. Virginia raiding parties scoured the country on both sides of the Monongahela, seizing and beating men, frightening and abusing women, breaking houses and barns, plundering cellars, impressing grain and live stock and causing a general reign of terror. The long restrained animosities growing out of the boundary dispute now had play. Examples of the acts of violence have been preserved in letters written by the pioneers.

---

8 Pennsylvania Archives, vol. ix., pp. 193, 233, 304, 315, 332, 356, 367.

One of the men most vigorous in denouncing the Virginia proceedings and advising their neighbors to resist the draft was Captain John Hardin, who kept a grist mill near Redstone. His eldest son was Lieutenant John Hardin, of the Eighth Pennsylvania, afterward famous as General Hardin, of Kentucky. At the head of 40 or 50 horsemen, General Clark visited Hardin's settlement, announcing his purpose to hang the stubborn old pioneer. Hardin could not be found, but the Virginians caught one of his sons and kept him bound for several days. They broke open the mill, fed the grain to their horses, took possession of the dwelling, killed sheep and hogs for their food and feasted for three days at Hardin's expense. Then General Clark declared the old man's estate forfeited for treason, but was kind enough to give the property to the wife.[9]

A settler who visited one of Clark's camps made so bold as to say that the draft was illegal. He was arrested and confined in a log jail and Clark gave judgment that the man should be hanged in due course of time. The threat of execution was not carried out. It was merely one of the general's "bluffs," for which he was somewhat notorious. Some of the events of this time suggest that Clark had begun to drink pretty hard. He was in the home of Monongahela rye and the wealthier Virginia settlers were generous in their hospitality.

Colonel Gabriel Cox, who lived on Peter's creek, near Finleyville, went about with a band of armed men, drafting the reluctant settlers. He sought John Douglass, one of the newly elected magistrates for Washington county, but did not find him at home. Thinking to catch John in bed, Cox and his men returned to the house at night, burst in the door and frightened wife and children nearly to death. Douglass was not there and Cox threatened the trembling wife with his sword. The poor woman could not or would not tell where her husband was.

Colonel Marshel wrote to Philadelphia: "Cox and his

---

9 Pennsylvania Archives, vol. ix., pp. 343-345.
10 Pennsylvania Archives, vol. ix., p. 344; vol. x., p. 81.

party have taken and confined a considerable number of the inhabitants of this county; in a word, the instances of high treason against the state are too many to be enumerated.' Thomas Scott, an honored leader among the pioneers, wrote that Clark's conduct had been "highly oppressive and abusive," adding, "The particulars are numerous and horrid."[11] Christopher Hays and Scott wrote jointly, "The general's expedition has been wished well, and volunteers to that service have been encouraged, . . . but we have heartily reprobated the general's standing over these two counties with an armed force, in order to dragoon the inhabitants into obedience to a draft under the laws of Virginia."[12]

The factional contentions among the borderers caused the failure of Clark's expedition. The Virginia general mustered his forces at the mouth of Chartiers creek, a short distance below Pittsburg, and thence marched to Wheeling, where his boats were built. Above Wheeling the Ohio was too shallow in midsummer to permit of navigation. Clark waited at Wheeling at least two weeks, vainly expecting other additions to his band. Realizing, at length, that the army which he had hoped to lead could not be assembled, and that he must move, if at all, before his stock of provisions was seriously reduced or many of his volunteers had changed their minds, he embarked his men, on the morning of August 8, and began the descent of the Ohio river. His force numbered about 400, with Captain Craig's battery of three field pieces. Although his proud spirit would not permit him to give over his enterprise, he felt little confidence in its success. Just before his embarkation he wrote to Governor Jefferson, of Virginia, that he had "relinquished all expectation," adding, "I have been at so much pains that the disappointment is doubly mortifying."

Had General Clark waited but a few hours longer, his expedition might not have been entirely fruitless. In the

---

11 Pennsylvania Archives, vol. ix., p. 325.
12 Pennsylvania Archives, vol. ix., p. 355.

evening of the day in whose morning he departed from Wheeling, there arrived at that place, by overland march, about 100 volunteers from Westmoreland county, under the command of Colonel Archibald Lochry. These fine riflemen would have been a material addition to Clark's strength and a junction of forces would have avoided that grievous disaster which befell Lochry at the mouth of the little stream which has since borne his name.

At every opportunity on the voyage down the Ohio some of Clark's men ran away, and by the time he reached Fort Nelson, opposite Louisville, his force was wholly inadequate for a march into the Indian country. He remained in Fort Nelson several weeks, but before the cold weather came on most of his men dispersed and returned in small parties to their homes in Pennsylvania and Virginia."

---

13 Pennsylvania Archives, vol. ix., p. 333; Winsor's Westward Movement, p. 193; Frontier Forts, vol. ii., p. 194.

CHAPTER XXI.

LOCHRY'S DISASTER.

The destruction of Colonel Lochry's detachment, while it was trying to overtake General Clark, was the heaviest loss suffered by Westmoreland county during the Revolution. It involved about one hundred choice men of the border, including the energetic county lieutenant and half a dozen capable officers. In the spring of 1781 the General Assembly of Pennsylvania voted the formation of four companies of rangers, to be enlisted and employed in the northern and western counties for the remainder of the war. One of these companies was allotted to Westmoreland, and was raised by Captain Thomas Stokely. It was made up of experienced woodsmen, and, being intended for a permanent corps, was counted on to perform much better service in defense of the settlements than had been rendered by the small bodies of militia called out at intervals for short periods. This company, recruited to the number of 38, was involved in Lochry's disaster. Another party lost in this expedition was Captain Samuel Shannon's company of volunteers, about 20 strong, enlisted for four months for the frontier defense. Captain Robert Orr, of Hannastown, raised and equipped a small company of riflemen, and Captain William Campbell commanded a squad of horsemen.[1]

The militia officers of the county had directed Colonel

---
1 Pennsylvania Archives, vol. viii., pp. 749, 751; vol. ix., pp. 18, 28, 330; Western Annals, p. 332.

Lochry to raise 300 men for Clark's campaign, but only one-third of that number could be enlisted. The reluctance of the settlers to engage in an incursion into the Indian country grew out of the fact that their own homes were threatened daily. During the summer of 1781 the Indian raids into Westmoreland county were unprecedented in number and destructiveness. Many families deserted their improvements and sought safety east of the mountains, and most of those who stood their ground felt it to be their chief duty to protect their families and property. It was with great urging and exertion that Colonel Lochry secured nearly 100 men for the western campaign. It is probable that he ordered the companies of Stokely and Shannon into this special service, but the two other companies were strictly volunteer formations of militiamen. No evidence is found that Lochry resorted to the draft to raise his contingent.

Lochry's men were detained until the harvest was finished, but on August 1 they began to gather at Carnaghan's blockhouse, eleven miles northwest of Hannastown.[2] There the formal muster was held on the following day, and on Friday, August 3, the little band, under Colonel Lochry's command, began its march to join Clark at Wheeling. Only 83 men took the road. These were the pick of the frontier riflemen, but they were poorly provided for a campaign. Their chief article of food was flour, carried on horses. They were badly clothed, one writer saying that they were "in a manner naked." Before their arrival at Wheeling, they were joined by a few additional men, so that the entire force was nearly 100.

The first camp was at Gaspard Markle's mill, on Big Sewickley creek, two miles east of West Newton. At that place Lochry received, by a fast-riding express, a letter from the president of Pennsylvania, approving Westmoreland's participation in Clark's enterprise. In reply to this,

---

2 For the details of the expedition see Lieutenant Isaac Anderson's Journal, in Pennsylvania Archives, Second Series, vol. xiv. Also Frontier Forts, vol. ii., p. 334; Pennsylvania Archives, First Series, vol. ix., p. 369.

before marching in the morning, Lochry wrote his last letter that has been preserved, saying therein: "I am now on my march with Captain Stokely's company of rangers and about 50 volunteers from this county. We shall join General Clark at Fort Henry. . . . I expected to have had a number more volunteers, but they have by some insinuations been hindered from going."[3]

The determined little band did not travel by way of Fort Pitt. It crossed the Youghiogheny at the site of West Newton, crossed the Monongahela at Devore's ferry, where Monongahela City now is; went overland by the settlements on the headwaters of Chartiers and Raccoon creeks, and reached Fort Henry in the evening of Wednesday, August 8. Here was a disappointment. General Clark had departed by boats that morning. To prevent the desertion of his men, he had found it necessary to remove farther from the settlements, and he left a message that he would wait for Lochry at the mouth of the Little Kanawha. But Lochry had no boats and could not follow immediately. For four days he was detained at Wheeling while seven boats were built, and these four days were fatal.

From the mouth of the Little Kanawha Clark's men began to desert, cutting across through the woods toward the settlements on the Monongahela, and to prevent the entire breaking up of his small force the general was compelled to move on down the river.

On August 13 Lochry's boats were ready and most of his men embarked in them, while the horses were conducted along shore. At this time the Ohio river was the dividing line between the white man's country and the Indian's. The boats kept near the southern shore and all encampments were on the left bank. Although Colonel Lochry and his men did not know it, they were watched by Indian spies following them through the forests and thickets on the farther shore, keeping in touch by swift runners with the Indian chiefs on the Scioto and the Miamis. On those

---

3 Pennsylvania Archives, First Series, vol. ix., p. 333.

streams the red warriors were gathering to resist Clark's advance, and a greater chief than any among the Ohio tribes had come with his Mohawks from Central New York to fight the white invaders.

At Fishing creek Lochry met 17 men who had deserted from Clark and were trying to make their way to Fort Pitt. These he forced to join his party. At the Three Islands, below the Long Reach, Lochry found Major Charles Crascraft and six men who had been left by Clark in charge of a large horse boat for Lochry's animals. Into this boat the horses were put, and after that the party was able to move with increased speed. Crascraft did not remain with Lochry, but in a skiff hurried away after Clark.

On the following day, August 16, Colonel Lochry sent Captain Shannon and seven men in a small boat, to endeavor to overtake Clark and beg him to leave some provisions for the Westmoreland men. Lochry's flour was almost exhausted, and food could be secured only by sending out hunters, whose excursions delayed progress. On August 17 two men who were sent out to hunt did not return, and they were never heard of. It is probable they were killed by Indians.

Three days later two of Captain Shannon's men, half starved, were picked up from the southern shore. They told a story of the first disaster. Their little party had landed on the Kentucky side, below the mouth of the Scioto, to cook a meal, and the two survivors, with a sergeant, had gone out to hunt. When they were about half a mile in the woods they heard the firing of guns in the direction of their camp. They had no doubt that Indians had fallen upon Shannon and his four companions, and, being too badly frightened to return to the river bank to investigate, they immediately set out up stream to rejoin Lochry. In scrambling through the underbrush the sergeant's knife fell from its sheath, and, sticking upward in the bush, the sergeant instantly trod upon its keen point. The blade passed through his foot, and the unfortunate man died in a few hours, after suffering great agony.

The direst result of this calamity was not the death of the captain and his men, but the capture from them of a letter from Lochry to Clark, revealing the weakness of Lochry's party and its distressed condition. Through this information the fate of the Westmoreland men was sealed.

Lochry was now fully aware that both shores of the river were beset by savages, and for two days and nights no landing or halt was made. The little flotilla passed swiftly down the stream. But this could not be long continued. It became absolutely necessary to land somewhere, to feed the horses and seek meat for the men.

In the forenoon of Friday, August 24, the boats approached a quiet and charming level spot at the mouth of a little creek on the Indian shore. This stream has since been called Lochry's run. It is the dividing line between Ohio and Dearborn counties, in the southeastern corner of Indiana. On that quiet summer morning it seemed to be the abode of eternal peace. The river was low, and a long sandbar, reaching out from the Kentucky shore, compelled the boats to pass close to the level spot on the northern bank. A buffalo was drinking at the river's edge, and one of the riflemen brought it down. Colonel Lochry at once ordered a landing, for here was meat for his hungry men and luxuriant grass for his horses. The boats were beached and men and horses were soon ashore.

Suddenly half a hundred rifles blazed from the wooded bank that flanked the little strip of meadow. Some of the whites were instantly killed and others wounded. The men made for the boats and many got into them, shoving off toward the southern shore. Painted savages then appeared, shrieking and firing, and a fleet of canoes, filled with other savages, shot out from the Kentucky shore, completely cutting off the escape of the white men. The Westmorelanders returned the fire for a minute or two, but were fatally entrapped, and Colonel Lochry stood up and called out a surrender. The combat ceased, the boats were poled back to shore and the little force landed a second time. Human blood was now mingled with that of the buffalo in the languidly flowing river.

The Westmoreland men found themselves the prisoners of Joseph Brant, the famous war chief of the Mohawks, with a large band of Iroquois, Shawnees and Wyandots. George Girty, a brother of Simon, was in command of some of the Indians. The fierce Shawnees could not be controlled, and began at once to kill their share of the prisoners. While Lochry sat on a log a Shawnee warrior stepped behind him and sank his tomahawk into the colonel's skull, tearing off the scalp before life was gone. It was with great difficulty that Brant prevented the massacre of the men assigned to the Mohawks and Wyandots.

About 40 of the Westmorelanders were slain, most of them after the surrender. The captives whose lives were spared numbered 64. Among those who escaped death were Captains Stokely and Orr, the latter being severely wounded in the left arm.[4]

The mutilated dead were left unburied on that lovely spot beside the Ohio, and the prisoners were hurried away into the Indian country. Some of them were scattered among the savage tribes, but most of them were taken by the Mohawks to Detroit, where they were given up to Major DePeyster, the British commandant. They were transferred to a prison in Montreal. From that place a few escaped and the remainder were released and sent home after the treaty of peace between Great Britain and the United States.

As far as the records show, the following were the only members of this expedition who returned to their homes in Westmoreland:[5]

Richard Wallace, of Fort Wallace, who was quartermaster to Colonel Lochry.

Captain Thomas Stokely, Lieutenant Richard Fleming, Robert Watson, John Marrs, Michael Hare, John Guthrie,

---

[4] Pennsylvania Archives, vol. ix., p. 458; Washington-Irvine Correspondence, p. 67; Western Annals, p. 333; The Girtys, p. 129; Hist. Collections of Pa., p. 97; Winsor's Westward Movement, p. 193.

[5] Pennsylvania Archives, First Series, vol. ix., pp. 574, 733; Colonial Records of Pa., vol. xiii., pp. 325, 473; Pennsylvania Archives, Second Series, vol. xiv.

John Scott, James Robinson, James Kane, John Crawford, Peter McHarge and James Dunseath.

Lieutenant Isaac Anderson, of Captain Shannon's company.

Ezekiel Lewis, of Captain Campbell's company.

Captain Robert Orr, Lieutenant Samuel Craig, Jr., Ensign James Hunter and Manasseh Coyle.

James McPherson, one of the captives, accepted British service, and acted with the Indians on the northwestern border until after Wayne's victory in 1794.[6]

---

[6] Howe's Historical Collections of Ohio, vol. ii., p. 104.

CHAPTER XXII.

MORAVIANS AND WYANDOTS.

For some time before his fatal journey, Colonel Lochry had been losing favor with the Supreme Executive Council in Philadelphia. No question was raised concerning his sincerity and energy in the patriot cause, but his failures to co-operate with Colonel Brodhead, his tardiness and irregularity in rendering accounts of his large public expenditures and the looseness of his militia discipline were charged against him openly. A secret cause of dissatisfaction was his personal antagonism to Colonel Christopher Hays, who wielded at that time a stronger political influence in Philadelphia than any other resident of Westmoreland. Early in the summer Hays was authorized by President Reed to consult with Thomas Scott and other close friends on the frontier and to nominate a successor to Lochry.[1]

On August 15, 1781, while Colonel Lochry was descending the Ohio to his death, Hays and Scott, in a joint letter to President Reed, nominated Edward Cook for county lieutenant[2] and the nomination was confirmed by the Supreme Council before the news was received that the office had been rendered vacant by the blow of a Shawnee's tomahawk. Edward Cook was one of the notable men of early Westmoreland. He was born at Chambersburg, Pa., in 1741, and at the age of 30 settled between the Monongahela and the Youghiogheny in what is now Wash-

---
1 Pennsylvania Archives, vol. ix., pp. 301, 307.
2 Pennsylvania Archives, vol. ix., pp. 354, 440.

ington township, Fayette county. In 1772 he built the first stone mansion in that region and built it so stoutly that it is still occupied by his descendants. His plantation comprised 3,000 acres, fronting on the Monongahela and including the land now occupied by Fayette City. He owned many slaves, was a man of large wealth and famous hospitality and exercised the most extensive influence throughout the Monongahela valley. He was a ruling elder of the Presbyterian church and the chief founder of the pioneer congregation of Rehoboth. He became a member of the committee of correspondence of Westmoreland county and was a delegate to the convention of 1776, which formed the first state constitution of Pennsylvania. For more than four years he was a sub-lieutenant under Lochry.

Another important change took place on the frontier in the fall of 1781. Several times Colonel Brodhead had been involved in quarrels, not only with the local militia officers, but with members of his own staff at Forts Pitt and McIntosh; and when he was accused by Alexander Fowler, a Pittsburg merchant, who had been appointed to audit the military accounts in the West, of speculating with public money, the officers insisted that he should resign his command to Colonel John Gibson, the next in rank. Although a court-martial had been ordered to try him, Brodhead declined to retire, and made it necessary for Washington to write to him under date of September 6, to turn over his command to Colonel Gibson.[3] Brodhead obeyed this order on September 17 and departed for Philadelphia. He was acquitted of the charges against him and for many years afterward occupied offices of trust and profit in Pennsylvania. He died in 1809 and was buried at Milford, Pa.

His successor in the command of the Western Department was Brigadier General William Irvine, appointed by Congress on September 24, 1781.[4] He was a native of Ireland, of Scotch descent, a graduate of the University of

---
3 Washington-Irvine Correspondence, p. 62.
4 Pennsylvania Archives, vol. ix., pp. 419, 425, 433.

Dublin and had served for a short season as a surgeon of the British navy. At the close of the Seven Years War he quit the service, emigrated to Pennsylvania and became a physician in the town of Carlisle. He attained a local eminence and some degree of fortune, took a leading part in the patriotic agitation of 1774, was a member of the provincial convention of that year which recommended a general congress and afterward gave his attention to the organization of the Cumberland county associators or "minute men." In January, 1776, he was appointed colonel of the Sixth Pennsylvania, formed his regiment and marched through New York to participate in the invasion of Canada. At the battle of Three Rivers, June 16, 1776, he was captured, was released on parole seven weeks later, but was compelled to remain out of the service until May 6, 1778, when he was exchanged. As colonel of the Second Pennsylvania and brigadier general in the Pennsylvania line, he served with distinction under General Wayne in New Jersey and was in several sharp engagements. When he was ordered to Ft. Pitt he was 40 years old and was the most capable and accomplished officer in command of the Western Department during the war.

General Irvine arrived at Ft. Pitt about the first of November, 1781, and set to work energetically to introduce system into the several branches of the military service, to restore discipline among the troops and to conciliate the factions among the settlers and militiamen of the frontier. It was his good fortune to be able to signalize his assumption of command by a public celebration of the surrender of Cornwallis, which had taken place at Yorktown on October 19.

Just before the arrival of General Irvine in the West, an event took place in the valley of the Tuscarawas river, which entailed many evil results to the frontier. A large body of savages forcibly removed the Moravian missionaries and their Indian converts from their three settlements on the Tuscarawas to the valley of the Sandusky, where they were planted amid the villages of the hostile Wyandots and Delawares.

This removal was ordered, with good reason, by Colonel DePeyster, the British commandant at Detroit. The presence of the Moravians almost midway between the British and the American posts had seriously interfered with the prosecution of the war by the British and Indians against the colonies. The missionaries and their converts claimed a strict neutrality but did not observe it. Zeisberger and Heckewelder were secretly the friends of the Americans and conducted a regular clandestine correspondence with the officers at Ft. Pitt, giving valuable information of the movements of the British and hostile savages. This correspondence was suspected by DePeyster and his partisan leaders and they had several times urged the Moravians to move nearer to Detroit. The hostile Indians threatened the converts with destruction because they would not join in the war, while many of the borderers believed that the men of the Tuscarawas villages did occasionally participate in raids on the settlements. The settlers had little or no faith in the Christianity of the Moravian red men. To save the Moravians from danger on both sides, Colonel Brodhead advised them to take up their residence near Ft. Pitt, but they refused to heed his warnings. The convert villages were between two fires, constantly liable to be consumed by one or the other, but Zeisberger and Heckewelder were blind to the peril.

In August, 1781, DePeyster became convinced that the missionaries were giving information to the Americans. Thereupon he sent Captain Matthew Elliott, with a small party of tories and French-Canadians, to secure Indian assistance and remove the Moravians to the Sandusky. Elliott was joined by about 250 savages, including Wyandots, under Dunquat, the half-king; Delawares, led by Captain Pipe, and a few Shawnees.[5] Elliott's party performed its errand with unnecessary harshness.

The Moravian Indians numbered about one hundred families[6] and occupied three villages on the Tuscarawas

---
5 The Girtys, p. 132.
6. Ft. Pitt, p. 240.

river. Schoenbrun (Beautiful Well) was on the west bank of the stream, two miles below the present town of New Philadelphia. Seven miles farther down the river, on the eastern bank, was the principal village, Gnadenhuetten (Tents or Huts of Grace), and again on the western bank, five miles farther down, was Salem.[7] These villages consisted of fairly comfortable log cabins and were surrounded by vegetable gardens and large fields of maize. The Indians possessed herds of cattle and hogs and many horses.

Elliott's band seized and confined the missionaries and their families and gathered them and all the converted Indians at Gnadenhuetten. The prisoners were permitted to prepare food for the journey and to pack up some of their goods, but their huts were looted and many things were stolen by the hostiles. On September 11 the movement from Gnadenhuetten began. Blankets, furs, utensils and provisions were carried on the horses and the cattle were driven along, but the Moravians were forced to leave behind their great stock of corn, unhusked in the fields. Men, women and children trudged afoot, and the feeble ones, white and red, suffered sorely from fatigue and hunger.

The sad procession descended the Tuscarawas to its junction with the Walhonding and passed up the latter stream to its sources, thence over the dividing ridge to the Sandusky. In the ascent of the Walhonding the greater part of the provisions was conveyed in canoes, and during a wild rain storm two of these canoes were sunk, with their valuable cargoes.[8]

By the time the Moravians had reached the Sandusky river they had been robbed of their best blankets and cooking vessels and their food was exhausted. On the east side of the stream, about two miles above the site of Upper Sandusky, they settled down in poverty and privation, built rude shelters of logs and bark and spent a winter of great distress.

In the following March the missionaries were taken, by order of DePeyster, to Detroit for a second time, where

---

7 Historical Collections of Ohio, vol. ii., p. 682.
8 Western Annals, p. 373; Westward Movement, p. 194; Taylor's History of Ohio, Cincinnati, 1854, p. 357.

they were closely examined on the charge of having corresponded with the Americans at Ft. Pitt.[9] Although they were guilty of this charge, the evidence was not at hand to convict them. DePeyster treated them kindly but would not permit them to return to the Sandusky. They were compelled to make a new settlement on the Huron river.

A striking incident in the history of Washington county was connected with the removal of the Moravians. While the exiles were being conducted up the Walhonding, seven Wyandot warriors left the company and went on a raid across the Ohio river. Among the seven were three sons of Dunquat, the half-king, and the eldest son, Scotosh, was the leader of the party. They crossed the Ohio on a raft, which they hid in the mouth of Tomlinson's run. They visited the farm of Philip Jackson, on Harman's creek, and captured Jackson in his flax field. The prisoner was a carpenter, about 60 years old, and his trade made him valuable to the Indians, as he could build houses for them. The savages did not return directly to their raft, but traveled by devious ways to the river, to baffle pursuit. The taking of the carpenter was seen by his son, who ran nine miles to Ft. Cherry, on Little Raccoon creek, and gave the alarm. Pursuit the same evening was prevented by a heavy rain, but the next morning seventeen stout young men, all mounted, gathered at Jackson's farm. Most of the borderers decided to follow the crooked and half obliterated trail, but John Jack, a professional scout, declared that he believed he knew where the Indians had hidden their raft and called for followers. Six men joined him, John Cherry, Andrew Poe, Adam Poe, William Castleman, William Rankin and James Whitacre, and they rode on a gallop directly for the mouth of Tomlinson's run.

Jack's surmise was a shrewd one, based on a thorough knowledge of the Ohio river and the habits of the Indians. At the top of the river hill the borderers tied their horses in a grove and descended cautiously to the river bank. At the mouth of the run were five Indians, with their prisoner, preparing to shove off their raft. John Cherry fired the first

---

9 The Girtys, p. 145.

shot, killed an Indian, and was himself killed by the return fire. Four of the five Indians were slain, Philip Jackson was rescued without injury, and Scotosh escaped up the river with a wound in his right hand.

Andrew Poe, in approaching the river, had gone aside to follow a trail that deviated to the left. Peering over a little bluff, he saw two of the sons of the half-king sitting by the stream. The sound of the firing at the mouth of the run alarmed them and they arose. Poe's gun missed fire and he jumped directly upon the two savages, throwing them to the ground. A fierce wrestling contest took place. Andrew Poe was six feet tall, of unusual strength and almost a match for the two brothers. One of them wounded him in the wrist with a tomahawk, but he got possession of the only rifle that was in working order and loaded, and fatally shot the one who had cut him. Poe and the other savage contested for the mastery, awhile on the shore and then in the water, where Andrew attempted to drown his antagonist. The Indian escaped, reached land and began to load his gun, when Andrew struck out for the opposite shore, shouting for his brother Adam. At the opportune moment, Adam appeared and shot the Indian through the body, but before he expired the savage rolled into the water and his corpse was carried away down the stream. One of the borderers, mistaking Andrew in the stream for an Indian, fired at him and wounded him in the shoulder. The triumphant return of the party to Ft. Cherry was saddened by the death of John Cherry, who was a man of great popularity and a natural leader on the frontier.[10]

Scotosh, the only survivor of the raiding band, succeeded in swimming the Ohio and hid over night in the woods. In the morning he made a small raft, recrossed the stream, recovered the body of his brother lying on the beach, conveyed it to the Indian side of the river and buried it in the woods. He then made his way to Upper Sandusky, with a sad message for his father and the tribe.[11]

---

10 The account of this affair is based principally upon the Narrative of Adam Poe, grandson of the original Adam Poe, published in serial form in the East Liverpool (O.) Crisis, during July and August, 1891.
11 The Girtys, pp. 134, 151.

CHAPTER XXIII.

THE SLAUGHTER AT GNADENHUETTEN.

In the fall of 1781, Pennsylvania frontiersmen decided that their safety would no longer permit the residence of the Moravians on the Tuscarawas. Even if it were not true that the mission Indians sometimes went on the war trail, it was certain that they gave food and shelter to war parties. Colonel David Williamson, one of the battalion commanders of Washington county, gathered a company of from 75 to 100 men and rode to the Tuscarawas in November, with the purpose of compelling the Moravians either to migrate into the hostile country or to move in a body to Ft. Pitt. This company discovered what Captain Elliott and his Indians had accomplished two months earlier. They found the mission villages deserted save by a few Indian men and women who had wandered back from the Sandusky to gather corn. Williamson conducted these Indians safely to Ft. Pitt and placed them under the care of General Irvine. Food being scarce at the fort, Irvine did not keep the Indians long, but permitted them to go to their brethren on the Sandusky.[1]

Already a small settlement of Delawares had been established near Ft. Pitt. After Colonel Brodhead destroyed Coshocton in the spring of 1781, Killbuck, the chief sachem of the Delaware tribe, with his immediate kindred and the families of Big Cat, Nanowland and a few other chiefs who remained friendly to the American cause, took

---
1 Crumrine's History of Washington County, p. 102.

possession of a small island at the mouth of the Allegheny river, opposite Ft. Pitt, built bark wigwams, grew corn and vegetables and otherwise supported themselves by the chase and the sale of furs. Members of this settlement on what was called Killbuck island—afterward Smoky island—accompanied military scouting parties and were of service in the defense of the frontier. Killbuck was a colonel in the United States army and some of his men received commissions as captains.

The spring of 1782 was unusually early. Mild weather began about the first of February and with it came the marauding Indians. The first blow in Southwestern Pennsylvania fell on February 8, when John Fink, a young man, was killed near Buchanan's fort, on the upper Monongahela.[2] On Sunday, February 10, a large body of Indians visited the dwelling of Robert Wallace, on Raccoon creek. The head of the family was away from home. The savages killed his cattle and hogs, plundered the cabin of household utensils, bedding, clothing and trinkets, and carried away Mrs. Wallace and her three children, a boy of 10 years, another boy of 3 years, named Robert, and an infant.[3]

In the evening Robert Wallace returned to his desolated home. He ran and told his neighbors and in the morning an effort was made to follow the trail; but snow had fallen and obliterated the tracks. Enough was seen around the cabin to show that the Indians numbered about forty.

These raids, much earlier in the year than usual, greatly alarmed and perplexed the settlers. They could scarcely believe that the savages had come all the way from the Sandusky so quickly, and suspicion arose that hostile Indians had taken possession of the deserted cabins on the Tuscarawas.

About the 15th of February six Indians captured John Carpenter with two of his horses on the Dutch fork of Buf-

---

[2] Pennsylvania Archives, First Series, vol. ix., p. 496; Crumrine, p. 103; Withers's Chronicles of Border Warfare, pp. 232, 233.
[3] Pennsylvania Archives, vol. ix., p. 511; The Girtys, p. 154; Crumrine, pp. 103, 104; Washington-Irvine Correspondence, p. 101.

falo creek. They crossed the Ohio at Mingo Bottom and made off with him toward the Tuscarawas villages. Four of the captors were Wyandots but the other two spoke Dutch and told Carpenter they were Moravians. On the morning of the second day after crossing the river, Carpenter was sent into the woods to get the horses. He found them at some distance from the campfire, mounted one of them, on a sudden impulse, and rode hard for liberty. He struck the Ohio near Ft. McIntosh, went thence up to Ft. Pitt, where he told his story to Colonel Gibson, and then returned to his home in the Buffalo creek settlement.[4]

Colonel Marshel, the county lieutenant, had already called out some of the militia for the frontier defense, but when Carpenter told what he had learned, that a large body of Indians was on the Tuscarawas and that Moravians were among the border raiders, it was determined to muster more men and destroy the Tuscarawas valley villages as harboring places for the "red vipers." The young men of Washington county turned out to the number of 160, all well mounted, and Colonel Williamson was placed in command. With much difficulty the force crossed the swollen Ohio to the Mingo Bottom on the morning of Monday, March 4, and pursued the well-beaten trail leading toward Gnadenhuetten. In this expedition Robert Wallace was an eager volunteer.

Not far from the river the horsemen came upon a spectacle that aroused their fiercest indignation. Beside the trail, impaled upon the sharpened trunk of a sapling, was the naked and torn corpse of Mrs. Wallace. Nearby lay the mutilated body of her hapless infant. Imagine, if possible, the grief and rage of the husband and father and the stern oaths with which his rough companions pledged themselves to execute his cries for vengeance. On the border of the forest the bodies of the poor victims were buried and the grim-visaged frontiersmen remounted their horses and hurried their course onward along the trail of the murder-

---

4 The Girtys, p. 155; Crumrine, p. 103; Washington-Irvine Correspondence, pp. 101, 102.

ers. In the evening of March 6 the cavalcade was within striking distance of Gnadenhuetten and scouts brought back the news to the night camp that the once deserted town was again full of Indians. There could not be much doubt in the minds of Williamson's men that the red fiends whom they were seeking were in the village before them and that vengeance should be executed in the morning.

As a matter of fact, nearly all the temporary occupants of Gnadenhuetten and the two other Moravian villages were mission Indians from the Sandusky, who had come back to their old homes to gather their corn. Some of them had left the Sandusky as early as the middle of January, and others had followed in small parties, until about 150 men, women and children were in the Tuscarawas valley by the beginning of March.[5] Not all the men who made this journey were mission Delawares. At least ten of them were Wyandot warriors,[6] who halted but a short time at Gnadenhuetten and then proceeded on their way to pillage the settlements east of the Ohio. All the circumstances of the time, the many tracks seen in the Raccoon valley, the narrative of John Carpenter and the subsequent discoveries in the Tuscarawas villages, show that these Wyandot warriors were accompanied in their raiding by a considerable number of the Moravian Indian men, whose savage instincts were not entirely destroyed by the teachings of the missionaries. The women and the children had been left to do the corn gathering, with some of the men too old to go upon the war trail.

Colonel Williamson's cautious plan for the capture of Gnadenhuetten indicates that he believed the town to be occupied by hostile warriors. He divided his force into three parties, sending one company to strike the river below the town, a second to cross the stream above and cut off retreat in that direction, while the third company, forming the center, should advance upon the place directly. The attack was made in the morning of March 7 and not a shot was

---

5 The Girtys, p. 154.
6 Pennsylvania Archives, vol. ix., p. 540.

fired by the center or the left. The presence of women and children warned the frontiersmen, when they came within view of the village, that it was not occupied simply by a war party, and Colonel Williamson quickly learned that the Indians were Moravians. No resistance was made, there was no show of hostile action and white men and red were soon mingling freely. A few of the Indian men spoke English. With these Colonel Williamson held council and told them that they must go to Ft. Pitt instead of returning to Sandusky. The Indians appeared to be willing to accept this new destination, and, at the colonel's suggestion, they sent messengers down the river to Salem, to tell the people there to come to Gnadenhuetten.

The men composing the right wing of Williamson's command had a more stirring experience. They found the Tuscarawas in flood and with so swift a current that they could not trust their horses to it. A young man of the name of Sloughter swam the stream to get what he took to be a canoe, but which turned out to be a "sugar trough," a half log hollowed out as a receptacle for maple water. He pushed it back to the eastern shore, and with the help of this trough nearly a score of the borderers crossed the river. Each man stripped, placed his clothing and rifle in the trough and pushed it before him as he swam. Advancing afoot down the western shore, toward corn fields where Indians had been seen at work, a solitary Indian was encountered and was instantly fired at. He was wounded in the arm, and as the white men rushed upon him he called out that he was a friend and the son of Shebosh (a Moravian preacher). Charles Bilderback slew the half-breed with a tomahawk and tore off the scalp. This act was seen by another Indian called Jacob, who sought to slip away unseen to a canoe he had hidden by the river bank. He was espied by some of the raiders and shot dead on the shore. His body was pushed into the river and floated away with the flood.[7]

---

[7] Heckewelder's Narrative of the Mission of the United Brethren, pp. 320, 321; Crumrine, p. 105; Historical Collections of Ohio, vol. ii., p. 684.

The company advanced upon the Indians in the corn field, discovered in some way that they were Moravians, made friends with them and conducted them to Gnadenhuetten. Soon afterward the party from Salem arrived, so that the whole number of Indians assembled was not less than 96. They were confined in the log church, after the Indian men had all been disarmed, even to their pocketknives.

While the Indians were being assembled and conducted to the church, certain discoveries were made which confirmed the first suspicions of the borderers and again excited their anger and passion for revenge. One of the Indian women was found to be wearing the dress of Mrs. Wallace. The garment was identified by the bereaved husband. A search of the cabins resulted in the finding of household utensils apparently stolen from the settlements. Some of them were recognized by Robert Wallace as his own property.[8] The volunteers immediately began to clamor for the death of the prisoners. Williamson withstood their demand and consulted his captains. Some of them favored the execution of the whole band. It appears that a long council was held and that many of the Indian men were brought before it, one at a time, and closely examined. Not one of them acknowledged his own guilt but confessions were made that some of the prisoners had been upon the war path. In a few cases the trimming of the hair and paint upon the face indicated that the men were warriors.[9] These revelations produced such an effect upon the frontiersmen that the colonel was no longer able to resist the outcry for vengeance. He put the question to vote whether the prisoners should be taken to Ft. Pitt or put to death on the spot, and it is recorded that only 18 of the whole body of volunteers stood up for mercy. It was decided to slay all the Indians in the morning.

Bishop Loskiel in his History of the Mission of the United Brethren,[10] says that the prisoners

---
8 Crumrine, p. 106.
9 The Girtys, p. 157.
10 Loskiel's History, vol. iii., pp. 177 to 182.

were informed in the evening of their condemnation and that they spent the night in praying, singing hymns and exhorting one another to die with the fortitude of Christians. His precise narrative of the things said and done by the captives in the little church during that night of agony must be largely the product of imagination.

In the morning of Friday, March 8, the decree of condemnation was executed. The Indian men were led, two by two, to the cooper shop and there beaten to death with mallets and hatchets. Some of them died praying; others strode to their doom chanting the savage war song. Two broke away and ran for the river, but were shot dead. The women and children were led into another building and slain like the men. Not more than 40 of the raiders took part in these murders., There were slaughtered, on that day, two score of men, a score of women and 34 children. It is probable that even the frontiersmen who stood aside and looked on did not consider this deed a crime. It was, in their view, justifiable retaliation for the almost numberless acts of outrage and murder perpetrated in the settlements by savage marauders through a series of bloody years. It was considered no worse to slay an Indian than to shoot a wolf, and the children of the red men were but wolf cubs, whose appetites and fangs were not yet developed.

From this massacre two Indian boys escaped. One hid himself in the cellar under the house where the women and children were butchered and crept forth after nightfall. The other was scalped among the men, but revived and crawled out to the woods under cover of darkness. They found each other in the forest and carried the horrid tale to the villages on the Sandusky.

During the day the militiamen gathered the plunder from the Indian cabins and found a goodly quantity of it, including pelts, blankets and a great store of corn in bags. A large party ascended the river to take and kill the Moravians in the village of Schoenbrun, but found not a soul there. Some Indians traveling from Schoenbrun toward Gnadenhuetten had come upon the scalped body of young

Shebosh, and, spying about Gnadenhuetten, had learned what was doing there. They had returned and warned their companions in Schoenbrun, and all who were there had escaped to the northward.

The cabins at Schoenbrun were burned, and during the ensuing night every building in Gnadenhuetten was consumed by fire, including the two slaughter houses with their heaped-up corpses. Salem was also destroyed and in the morning the frontiersmen departed on their march to the Ohio, with their booty loaded upon 80 horses taken from their Indian victims. At Mingo Bottom the spoil was divided among the raiders, who then scattered to their several settlements, big with stories of their famous victory.[11]

After they had been at home nearly two weeks, the militiamen who belonged in the Chartiers settlement assembled again and marched toward Pittsburg, to kill the Delawares who were living on Killbuck island. The attack was made on Sunday morning, March 24. On the island was an officer with a small guard of regular soldiers. These were surprised by the Chartiers men and made prisoners, and the Indians were then assailed. Several were killed, including Nanowland, the friend of Brady, and one other who held a captain's commission. Chief Killbuck and most of his band escaped in canoes to Ft. Pitt, where Colonel Gibson was in temporary command. Two of the warriors fled into the woods on the northern side of the river and made their way to Sandusky. One of these was the chief Big Cat, who was afterward a bitter and effective foe of the Americans. Before the Chartiers men returned home they sent word into Ft. Pitt that they would kill and scalp Colonel Gibson at the first opportunity, simply because he had been the protector of friendly Indians.[12]

General Irvine, who had been at Philadelphia and Carlisle, returned to Ft. Pitt on the day following the attack on the island and immediately took measures, by confer-

---

11 Washington-Irvine Correspondence, pp. 101, 102; Pennsylvania Archives, vol. ix., pp. 523 to 525.

12 Washington-Irvine Correspondence, pp. 100 to 103, 108; Ft. Pitt, p. 239.

ences with the militia officers of the neighboring counties, to put a stop to the criminal and reckless raids. A few weeks afterward he received an order from the Supreme Executive Council of Pennsylvania to investigate and report on the affair at Gnadenhuetten. He made diligent inquiry of the chief men of the frontier, including Colonel Williamson and some of his captains, but was unable to uncover all the details and responsibilities of the transaction. He soon learned that the sentiment of the border sustained the acts of Williamson's men and that any formal inquiry or attempt at punishment would be violently resisted. He was persuaded at length to report to Philadelphia that the precise facts could not be ascertained and that it would be wise to let the affair drop. That was the end of the matter.[13]

13 Pennsylvania Archives, vol. ix., pp. 525, 540, 541, 552; Washington-Irvine Correspondence, pp. 236-242, 245, 246. See Three Villages (Gnadenhuetten), by W. D. Howells, Boston, 1884; this publication is entertaining literature but not history.

CHAPTER XXIV.

CRAWFORD'S EXPEDITION AND DEATH.

The disgraceful exploit of David Williamson, at Gnadenhuetten, whetted the Scotch appetite for Indian blood. Although many frontiersmen approved Williamson's butchery of women and children, they felt, after all, that it was hardly a glorious deed, and it did not satisfy them as being a real revenge on their savage foes. A general desire was expressed for a campaign against Indians whose hostility was beyond question, and it was agreed that the blow ought to fall on the Wyandot and Delaware towns along the Sandusky river. A successful raid into that nest of vipers might obliterate the stain and obscure the recollection of Gnadenhuetten. So a general call went throughout the Washington county border, from Pittsburg to the Cheat river, for volunteers to invade again the land of the Indians and strike the savage tribes in one of their chief dwelling places.

This was not a militia movement. It did not issue from the county lieutenant or from any man in authority. It came from the leading men in the several centers of settlement, and met with a hearty response.[1] Through hard experience the borderers had become convinced that they must be their own defenders, and that the best way to protect their homes, their women and children, was to carry the war into the Indian country. They no longer relied on the garrison at Fort Pitt. They knew that garrison to

---
[1] Pennsylvania Archives, First Series, vol. ix., p. 540.

be too feeble and too miserably equipped to do any effective work. Moreover, the Scotch pioneers of Western Pennsylvania were by nature self-reliant. They were men of spunk, quite ready to do their own fighting in their own rough way.

The promoters of the movement requested General Irvine to lead them, but he declined to command a purely volunteer force and could spare no soldiers from his slender garrison. He was then asked to give to the expedition his approval and some little assistance. To this he agreed, requiring a pledge from the border leaders that they would furnish their own equipment and provisions, would conform to militia laws and regulations and would acknowledge their conquests as made in behalf of the United States. He furnished some gun-flints and a small supply of powder and detailed for the expedition Surgeon John Knight, of the Seventh Virginia, and one of his own aides, Lieutenant John Rose, a Russian nobleman, who served the American cause with singular fidelity, energy and ability.[2]

While the expedition was forming Indian ravages on the frontier became more virulent. The butchery on the Tuscarawas had stirred the savages to a fiercer hostility. Small war parties invaded Washington and Westmoreland counties and killed or captured many of the settlers in the immediate neighborhood of the companies of mustering yeomanry. Thomas Edgerton was captured on Harman's creek and John Stevenson near West Liberty. Five soldiers were ambushed in the woods near Ft. McIntosh; two were killed and the three others were taken to Lower Sandusky, where they successfully ran the gauntlet.[3] Two men were killed on the border of Washington county.[4] At Walthour's blockhouse, near Brush creek, in Westmoreland, a man of the name of Willard was killed and his daughter carried away and murdered in the woods.[5] On

---
2 Washington-Irvine Correspondence, pp. 113 to 117. The real name of John Rose was Henri Gustave Rosenthal.
3 The Girtys, p. 141; Ft. Pitt, p. 240; Historical Collections of Ohio, vol. ii., p. 531.
4 Pennsylvania Archives, vol. ix., p. 541.
5 Pa. Magazine of History and Biography, vol. i., pp. 46 to 48.

Sunday, May 12, Rev. John Corbly and his family, while walking to their meeting house on Muddy creek, in what is now Greene county, were attacked by savages. The preacher alone escaped without injury. The wife and three children were killed and scalped. Two daughters were scalped, but survived to endure years of suffering.[6]

The general muster was fixed for Monday, May 20, at Mingo Bottom, a beautiful level on the Ohio river, three miles below Steubenville. Edward Cook and James Marshel, the lieutenants of Westmoreland and Washington counties, had agreed that every man who joined this expedition, providing his own horse, gun and food, should be excused from two tours of militia duty. It was a cavalry force of Scotch farmers and their sons who trooped to the place of rendezvous during three or four days. By Friday 480 horsemen were assembled, who then proceeded to organize by electing officers.

Colonel William Crawford, who was at the time a regular officer of the Virginia line, was the principal candidate for the chief command, and, through the influence of General Irvine, was elected by five votes over David Williamson. The staff was chosen as follows: majors, David Williamson, Thomas Gaddis, John McClelland and John Brinton; brigade major, Daniel Leet. Major Rose served as adjutant, and the wilderness guides were Jonathan Zane, John Slover and Thomas Nicholson. Gaddis and McClelland were from Westmoreland county. The companies from the several communities attended under their own militia officers. Of some companies nearly all the members volunteered, while of others there were only ten or fifteen. In all, there were 18 companies, with the following captains: Josph Bane, John Beeson, John Biggs, Charles Bilderback, William Bruce, Timothy Downing, William Fife, John Hardin, John Hoagland, Andrew Hood, William Leet, Duncan McGeehan, John Miller, James Munn, Thomas Rankin, David Reed, Craig Ritchie and Ezekiel Ross.

---

6 Historical Collections of Pennsylvania, p. 359.
7 Washington-Irvine Correspondence, p. 114.

The rolls of this expedition show that nearly all of its members were of Scotch descent. With them were a few Irishmen and an occasional German was represented on the lists. It was on Saturday, May 25, that the expedition left the Ohio and followed the Indian trail toward the northwest. Almost from the beginning of the march the whites were watched by Indian spies, and swift runners bore the news to Sandusky and onward to Detroit. Crawford's expectation of success was based on a hope that he could surprise the Indian towns. This hope was not realized. The borderers were ten days riding to the Sandusky river, and in that time the savages had ample opportunity to prepare for battle. Their women and children were hurried away down the river, the warriors were summoned from the scattered villages and a body of British partisans came to their aid from Detroit. This force of white men consisted of a company of rangers under Lieutenant John Turney and Canadian volunteers commanded by Captain William Caldwell, somewhat exceeding 100 men. While Crawford was advancing leisurely his enemies were moving with remarkable celerity.

On the fourth day of their march the Pennsylvanians turned aside to visit the ruins of the Moravian town at Schoenbrun. They found little plunder there, but fed their horses on the standing corn. The entire distance traveled from the Ohio to Upper Sandusky was about 160 miles. The cavalcade reached the upper Indian town, on the Sandusky river, in the evening of Monday, June 3. The place was deserted and Colonel Crawford learned that the Indians had abundant warning of his approach. In view of this fact, Crawford advised a retirement[8], but a majority of the council decided to make another day's march, toward the principal Wyandot town. In the morning the command went forward, through the beautiful green plain on the west side of the Sandusky river, seeing no enemy until afternoon.

As they drew near to a large grove, standing like an

---
8 Pennsylvania Archives, vol. ix., p. 557.

island in the broad meadow, Crawford's men were saluted with a volley, and discovered the British and Indians darting among the trees. The Americans charged, drove their enemies from the covert and occupied the grove. The men dismounted, formed line along the northern side of the forest and for several hours exchanged a brisk fire with the British and Indians lying in the grass and bushes. Darkness closed the combat. In this first day's fight five Americans were killed and 19 wounded, while the enemy lost six killed and 11 wounded. One of the wounded was Captain Caldwell, the British commander.

During the night the savages howled and hooted all about the grove, and occasional shots allowed the frontiersmen little rest. When day came the Indians lay at a distance and the opposing sides engaged in long-range fighting. A band of Shawnee warriors, 140 in number, joined the foe in the afternoon. Their arrival was observed by the Americans, who were convinced that they were greatly outnumbered. As a matter of fact, however, the two forces were about equal. Toward evening the savages made a vigorous attack, but were repulsed. Crawford held another council of war and decided to retreat during the night. Watch fires were built along the edge of the grove, pickets were stationed in the shadows near them to discharge an occasional shot toward the enemy, and then, late in the night, the main body of Crawford's force began its silent retreat toward the Ohio.

Soon after the beginning of this night march one of the strange panics common in Indian warfare, seized upon the Scotch volunteers. On many occasions during the border wars bodies of ordinarily brave and well armed white men were affected by an unreasonable fear, especially during the night time, in the presence of savage foes, and fled away through the forest as if pursued by demons. This almost supernatural dread often turned victory into defeat. There is no other explanation for the unexpected retreats that followed many a good fight.

The silent retreat became a noisy one. Men called to

one another. Some fired their guns into the darkness. Others left the ranks and ran away, like insane men, across the pathless prairie. Then the savages came upon them in the night and began to slay and scalp the straggling fugitives. Many of the whites were without horses. Some of the animals had been shot; others had been lost. The retreat led into swamps where horses stuck fast and were deserted. A few of the men, weary of long fighting, had fallen asleep in the grove and were left behind. They awoke to find themselves deserted, and in little bands they set out, with no idea of direction, to escape from the savage terror. They heard the firing of guns to the southward and that sound they avoided. Some of them were overtaken and killed; others made their way to their homes after remarkable escapes and excessive hardships. The Indians ranged widely over the level country and glutted themselves with blood.

Among the members of the expedition were three of Colonel Crawford's kinsmen, John Crawford, his only son; William Crawford, a nephew, and William Harrison, a son-in-law. Not one of these could Colonel Crawford find. He stood by the trail, as the long line passed, and called for his son. No answer came and the colonel fell to the rear. He became lost, but met with Dr. Knight and nine other men. They wandered for two days and were then captured by a band of Delawares.

Colonel Williamson and Lieutenant Rose kept the main body of the Americans together. When day returned the panic subsided and order was restored. On the Olentangy, in the southern part of what is now Crawford county, the Delawares and Shawnees viciously assailed the rear guard, but the men stood firm and the savages were driven off with loss. After that the Indians did not molest the main force, but scattered in search of the many stragglers. Colonel Williamson reached the Ohio, at Mingo Bottom, on June 12, with about 300 men, and he safely brought home 20 of the wounded. During the succeeding two weeks other members of the expedition reached the settlements, singly or in bands of three and four. Ultimately the number of the missing was very small. Indeed, the killed did not exceed fifty during the whole campaign, and it is safe to say that at least half of these were slain by the Indians after they were made prisoners. In revenge for the deed at Gnadenhuetten, all of the prisoners were doomed to die. They were divided among the several villages and put to death with every device of savage ingenuity. So far as known, only two of the captives escaped from their tormentors. These were Dr. Knight, the Virginia surgeon, and John Slover, one of the guides.

Colonel William Crawford was burned at the stake in the valley of Tymoochee creek, about five miles west of Upper Sandusky. His torture was inflicted chiefly by women and children. It endured during four hours, in the presence of Dr. Knight, Captain Matthew Elliott and Simon Girty. The miserable man was tied by a long rope to a pole, his body was shot full of powder, his ears were cut off, burning faggots were pressed against his skin, he was gashed with knives. When he, at length, fell unconscious, his scalp was torn off and burning embers were poured upon his bleeding head. He arose, then, to his feet, began to walk around the pole, groaned and fell dead. The savages heaped fire upon his body, and it was consumed to ashes. Thus perished a man who had performed a prominent but not always a creditable part in the development of the frontier. Because he was the friend and land agent of Washington, he has been the object of praise he did not deserve.[9]

Crawford's son John, after perilous trials, reached home in safety, but William Crawford the younger and William Harrison were put to death by the Shawnees. Their bodies were cut to pieces and hung on poles. Dr. Knight saw nine prisoners killed by squaws. One old woman cut off the head of John McKinley, and it was kicked about like

---

9 Concerning the character of Crawford, see Washington-Irvine Correspondence, note to p. 115; Diary of David McClure, p. 108; St. Clair's letter to Gov. Penn, July 22, 1774, in St. Clair Papers, vol. i.

a football. Among others who met death were Captains John Biggs and John Hoagland, Major John McClelland and Lieutenant Ashley. All the officers were tortured, while the captured private soldiers were killed in a plain and unornamental manner. The melancholy result of the expedition encouraged the savages and brought upon the frontiers a still greater visitation of desolation.[10]

[10] By far the best narrative of this expedition is An Historical Account of the Expedition Against Sandusky, by C. W. Butterfield, Cincinnati, 1873. See also Roosevelt's Winning of the West, vol. ii.

CHAPTER XXV.

THE WOUNDED INDIAN.

Striking characteristics of border life during the Revolution were exhibited in the episode of the lame Indian. This was a Delaware warrior, wounded during a raid on a settlement, who surrendered at Fort Pitt to escape starvation and was afterward given up to a band of frontiersmen for execution. His story is rather an interesting one.

The settlement attacked was Walthour's station. It was a small stockade surrounding the log house of Christopher Walthour, on an elevated spot south of Brush creek, about a mile and a half east of Irwin. It was the chief rallying place for the Brush creek settlement, composed almost exclusively of German families, whose descendants are still numerous in that neighborhood. The Indian raid took place in April, 1782. Depredations by the savages had already been committed in several parts of Westmoreland county and the families of the farmers were gathered for refuge in the stockades scattered about the frontier. From these stockades the men issued in small parties, well armed, to perform the necessary work of planting the crops. Near Walthour's station half a dozen men were at work in a field. Among them was a son-in-law of Christopher Walthour, of the name of Willard, whose daughter, 16 years old, was also with the party, probably for the purpose of carrying water to the men.

The workers were surprised by a band of Delawares, who captured the girl. The laborers seized their guns and made a running fight as they retired toward the fort in the face of superior numbers. Two of the white men were killed. One of them, Willard, fell not far from the stockade. An Indian rushed out of the bushes to scalp Willard, and was just twisting his fingers in the white man's long hair when a rifle bullet, fired from the fort, wounded the savage severely in the leg. The Delaware uttered a howl of pain and limped away into the thicket, leaving his gun behind him, beside the body of his victim.

As soon as a considerable band of frontiersmen could be collected, pursuit of the savages was undertaken. Their trail was followed to the Allegheny river, over which they had escaped into the Indian country. It was almost two months afterward when hunters found the decomposed body of the girl in the woods, not far from Negley's run. The head had been crushed with a tomahawk and the scalp was gone.

One evening, 38 days after the attack on Walthour's station, a lame Indian hobbled into the village of Pittsburg and made his way to the porch of one of the houses. He walked with the aid of a pole, and was, in appearance, a living skeleton. A young woman stepped forth to see him. He asked, feebly, for a drink, and she gave him a cup of milk. It was evident that he was nearly starved. After he had eaten ravenously of the food given to him, he told the members of the family, in broken English, that he had been hunting on Beaver river with a Mingo, who had quarreled with him and had shot him in the leg.

Word was sent to the garrison, and the Indian was taken down to the fort. There he was recognized as Davy, a Delaware sub-chief, who had often visited the fort. The surgeon discovered that the Indian's wound was an old one, and the officers told Davy that his story about the Mingo was plainly a lie.

After being treated tenderly and having recovered somewhat from his fatigue and hunger, the Indian confessed that he was the man who had killed Willard and had been wounded while trying to take the scalp. The shot had broken the bone of his leg and he was unable to keep up with his comrades when they fled. He had dragged himself into a dense thicket, where he lay in one spot for three days. During that time the settlers were scouring the woods and the wounded man was afraid to stir. When the pursuit was given up Davy crawled forth and sought for food. He found nothing but berries and roots and on such articles he lived for more than five weeks. They barely kept soul and body together and he was also weakened by the loss of blood from his painful wound. He made progress slowly toward the Allegheny river. He came within sight of a small stockade on Turtle creek and for a long time lay on a hill, meditating surrender. He finally satisfied himself that the garrison of the little fort consisted of militiamen and he knew that surrender to them meant death. The Indians were well aware of the difference between militia and regulars and knew that from the buck-skinned frontiersmen they could expect no mercy. Davy hobbled onward until he reached the Allegheny river.

On the bank of the river the wounded Indian lay for many days, finding scanty food while he watched for some of his countrymen. No one came and no possibility offered of his being able to cross the stream. Driven to desperation by hunger, he decided to make his way to Fort Pitt and give himself up to the regular soldiers.

Davy was confined in the guard house in the fort, in the expectation that opportunity might offer to exchange him for some white person held prisoner by the Indians. The news of his capture and his identity reached the settlement at Brush creek and caused considerable excitement there. The kindred and neighbors of the victims of the Indian raid were hot for revenge and now the chance for it was presented. Mrs. Mary Willard, the widow of the man whom Davy had killed, went to Fort Pitt in company with a party of neighbors and asked General Irvine to give up the prisoner, that he might be "properly dealt with" by those who had suffered.

At that time it was not known that Mrs. Willard's

daughter had been killed by her captors and the prospect was presented to the woman that Davy might be traded for her daughter. In the hope of such an arrangement Mrs. Willard consented that the Indian should remain some time longer at Ft. Pitt. But when the mutilated body of the girl was found, the people of Brush creek demanded the life of the captive savage. A mass meeting was held and a committee was chosen to go to Fort Pitt and renew negotiations with General Irvine for the surrender of the Indian. The members of this delegation were Joseph Studebaker, Jacob Byerly, Francis Byerly, Jacob Rutdorf, Henry Willard and Frederick Willard. The last two were probably brothers of the man who was slain.

Having many other things to worry him at that time, General Irvine yielded to the pleadings of the committee and surrendered the prisoner; but he compelled the delegates to agree to a method of procedure, which he hoped would save the Indian from abuse and torture. Here is the order of General Irvine given to the six frontiersmen:

"You are hereby enjoined and required to take the Indian delivered into your charge by my order and carry him safe into the settlement of Brush creek. You will afterward warn two justices of the peace, and request their attendance at such place as they shall think proper to appoint, with several other reputable inhabitants. Until this is done and their advice and direction had in the matter you are, at your peril, not to hurt him nor suffer any person to do it. Given under my hand at Fort Pitt, July 21, 1782.
"William Irvine."

At the same time the general sent a letter to Mrs. Willard, urging her to do nothing rashly in retaliating her vengeance on the prisoner and not to permit him to be put to death until after "some form of trial."

With great glee the borderers set their prisoner on a horse and conducted him to Walthour's. There preparations was made to burn him on the very spot where Willard died. The frontiersmen felt sure of the acquiesence of the two justices, for all through the settlements there was but one opinion as to the proper way to deal with Indians. Davy was placed in a log blockhouse for two or three days and nights, while word went out for the assembling of the magistrates and the settlers on a certain day. Then a form of trial was to be gone through with and the fiery execution was to be witnessed by the multitude.

On the night preceding the great day the young men who were stationed outside of the blockhouse to guard it all fell asleep. The one who first awoke in the morning peeped in to see if the prisoner was still there. The blockhouse was empty! The guard aroused his companions and an investigation quickly established the fact that Davy had actually escaped. The great door had been securely locked. No human being could go through one of the loopholes. There was but one way for escape, and that was through the narrow space between the overjutting roof and the top of the wall. It seemed almost impossible for the crippled savage to have climbed up the wall and squeezed through that opening, but there was no other way out of it.

Great was the disappointment and rage among the assembled settlers when they learned that their prey had escaped. In all directions eager searching parties ranged the country, but found not the wounded Delaware. For two days the hunt was maintained, but Davy had left no trail.

On the third day a lad who had gone into the wood to bring in some horses, ran almost breathless to Walthour's station and said that an Indian had stolen a gray mare. He had discovered the savage, who seemed to be crippled, mounting the mare from a large log. The Indian got astride, belabored the beast with a stout stick and went cantering off toward the Allegheny river.

Then the pursuit was taken up by a large body of men. The trail of the horse was followed with some difficulty. The Indian had ridden along the beds of shallow streams and on hard, stony places where the footprints were faint. But the tracks were followed patiently until they approached the river near the mouth of the Kiskiminetas. There the gray mare was found, covered with sweat, cropping grass in a glade near the water's edge, but no trace of the Indian was discovered. The river bank was searched for miles, up and down, but the frontiersmen were forced to return home empty handed.

A few years later, when peace had been restored, inquiries were made of members of the Delaware tribe concerning Davy's fate. He had never returned to his home. He had either been drowned while trying to swim the river, or had starved to death in the forest wilderness.[1]

---

[1] Frontier Forts, vol. ii., pp. 361 to 370; Washington-Irvine Correspondence, p. 384.

CHAPTER XXVI.

THE DESTRUCTION OF HANNASTOWN.

Hannastown, the county seat of Westmoreland, was destroyed by Indians on Saturday, July 13, 1782. This was the hardest blow inflicted by savages during the Revolution within the limits of the Western Pennsylvania settlements. It put an end to Hannastown, effacing it so thoroughly that thousands of the inhabitants of Westmoreland county do not know where its first county seat was located.

Hannastown was a little more than three miles northeast of Greensburg. It grew around the tavern of Robert Hanna, who set up a house of entertainment for travelers on the old Forbes road, some time before the Revolution. It never grew much, containing only about 30 log houses at the time of its destruction. One of the structures was the court house, two stories high, and another was the jail, only one story. At the northern end of the village a small stockade fort, made of pointed logs set upright, had been constructed in 1773, around a blockhouse and a spring. It was this fort, called Ft. Reed, that saved the villagers when the attack came.[1]

Hannastown and its neighborhood had suffered heavy loss in the preceding year by the destruction of Colonel Lochry's party on the lower Ohio. Many of the best men in the settlement had joined that expedition, and they carried with them most of the good guns. In 1782 the Han-

---

1 Ft. Pitt, p. 220, memorandum in General O'Hara's notebook.

nastown community was not in fit condition for defense against the Indians.

The blow that fell upon this frontier county seat came from the North. Early in the summer the Johnsons and the Butlers, the tory leaders of Western New York, gathered a strong force at Niagara to descend the Allegheny river and attack Fort Pitt. Three hundred British and Canadian soldiers and five hundred Indians, with twelve pieces of artillery, advanced to Lake Chautauqua and lay there while spies penetrated the neighborhood of Pittsburg. The report of these spies, that General Irvine had greatly strengthened the fort and increased its ordnance, caused the abandonment of the expedition, as far as its primary aim was concerned. Most of the British force returned to Niagara, but the Indians were not willing to go home without scalps and plunder. They divided into war parties, and went against the New York and Pennsylvania settlements.

The largest predatory band consisted of more than 100 Seneca warriors, under the command of Guyasuta, and about 60 Canadian rangers. Most of the white men were dressed and painted as Indians. This was the force that attacked and destroyed Hannastown. It descended the Allegheny river, partly in canoes and partly on horseback along shore,[2] to a point a short distance above Kittanning, left the canoes on the river bank and marched overland into the Westmoreland settlements. While the expedition was at its bloody work, many of the canoes worked loose and floated down the river. Several of them were picked up at Fort Pitt.

At that time the people of the frontier were in constant apprehension of Indian raids, but there was no expectation of an attack by a large band of savages. Men never went to their farm work without their rifles, but so long had the frontiersmen been exposed to alarms and dangers that they had grown indifferent and careless. Thus it occurred that at Miller's station, about two miles south of Hannastown,

---

2 Some of the raiders were mounted; see Wash.-Irvine Corr., p. 176.

men and women were gathered at a frolic, wholly unprepared to resist an attack.

On the Saturday when the blow fell, a party of harvesters was at work cutting the wheat of Michael Huffnagle, about a mile and a half north of Hannastown. Huffnagle was the county clerk and lived at the county seat. One of the harvesters, going to the edge of the field, discovered, creeping through the woods, a band of Indians, stripped and painted for war. He quietly informed his companions, and the harvesters, taking up their guns, fled unseen to the village.

The alarm was spread in the little settlement and everybody was warned to take refuge within the stockade. Great was the consternation and confusion. About 60 persons, men, women and children, were in the village that day, and most of these fled into the stockade without pausing to save any of their goods. Huffnagle and a few other men rescued the bulk of the county records and carried them safely into the fort. Sheriff Matthew Jack mounted his horse and rode away to warn the neighboring settlers, while four young men went out scouting, to observe the movements of the enemy. They came upon the savages advancing cautiously through the thick woods across the valley of Crabtree creek, and narrowly escaped capture. They fled back to the fort with the whole pack close at their heels. The Indians evidently expected to take the place by surprise, for they did not shoot or yell until they rushed in among the log houses. All the whites escaped except one man. He had lingered to gather up his personal property, and was slightly wounded before he reached the stockade gate.

About one hundred Indians and white men attacked Hannastown.[3] They drove into the woods all the horses found in the pasture lots and stables, killed a hundred cattle, many hogs and domestic fowls and plundered the deserted dwellings. Some of the white raiders threw off their jackets and donned better coats found in the houses,

---

3 Pennsylvania Archives, vol. ix., p. 596.

THE DESTRUCTION OF HANNASTOWN. 179

and after the assailants had retired several jackets were found bearing buttons of the King's Eighth regiment.

From the shelter of the cabins a hot rifle fire was opened on the stockade. The fort contained 20 men, who had 17 guns. It was found, however, that only nine of these were fit for use, and with this small number of weapons the men took turns at the loopholes. The main thing for them to do was to prevent the Indians from assaulting and battering the gates, and in this they were successful. The borderers were good marksmen, and kept the besiegers at a distance. It was certain that two of the Indians were killed, and the defenders believed that they killed or wounded several others.

But one person inside of the stockade was wounded. This was Margaret Shaw, 16 years old, who exposed herself before a large hole in one of the gates to rescue a child, which had toddled into danger. Margaret received a bullet in the breast, from which she died after suffering for nearly two weeks. She is buried a short distance north of Mt. Pleasant, and her memory should be kept green.

The firing on the fort continued until nightfall. Then the assailants set fire to the town, and danced and whooped in the glare of the flames. Only two houses escaped destruction. These were the court house and one cabin. Fire was set to them but went out, and as they stood near the stockade a renewal of the attempt to burn them was frustrated by the rifles of the frontiersmen. Fortunately the wind blew strongly from the north, and carried the flames and blazing embers away from the little fort.[4] After the buildings were well consumed, the savages and their white allies retired to the valley of Crabtree creek, where they feasted and reveled until a late hour. There was little sleep in the fort, and those who watched along the stockade heard the voices of white men mingling with those of the Indians in the enemy's camp.

A renewal of the attack was looked for in the morning,

---

4 Pennsylvania Archives, vol. ix., p. 606; Washington-Irvine Correspondence, pp. 176, 250, 251, 252; Frontier Forts, vol. ii., pp. 299 to 321.

but it did not come. Parties of horsemen from other settlements began to arrive early at the little fort, and when a reconnaissance of the creek valley was made, it was found that the enemy had slipped away. Guyasuta's raiders had departed with many stolen horses, laden with household goods, and they left a plain trail, but it was not until Monday that the borderers had the nerve to follow them, and then 60 men pursued the trail only to the crossing of the Kiskiminetas.

The enemy being gone, it was soon learned that great devastation had been inflicted in the surrounding country. A strong detachment of the savages had fallen upon Miller's station, two miles south of Hannastown, where they had killed eleven white persons and carried four into captivity. This station took its name from Samuel Miller, a captain in the Eighth Pennsylvania regiment, who was killed by the Indians in July, 1778.[5] His widow married Andrew Cruikshank, but the settlement retained Miller's name. A wedding took place at Cruikshank's house on July 12, and on the following day many persons were gathered there for the celebration. Upon this gay party the Indians swooped down.

The warning was barely sufficient to allow the escape of perhaps a dozen persons, who found hiding places in grain fields and forest thickets. Several men were shot dead while preparing for defense, and 15 men, women and children were taken prisoners. The houses were plundered and burned, and the Indians set out to rejoin their main force at Crabtree creek.

Among those taken captive were Lieutenant Joseph Brownlee, his wife and several children, Mrs. Robert Hanna and her daughter Jennie, a Mrs. White and two of her children. Lieutenant Brownlee had served in the Eighth Pennsylvania, but had been discharged because of a wound. As the prisoners were being driven through the woods, Mrs. Hanna addressed Brownlee as "Captain." The Indians at once fell upon Brownlee and killed him, as well

---

5 See page 72 of this work.

as a little son whom he was carrying, and nine others of the captives. Mrs. Brownlee and her infant and Mrs. Hanna and her daughter were spared and taken to Canada, but were afterward released when the war was over. Tradition says that Jennie Hanna married a British officer in Canada.[6]

On Sunday morning a band of Indians attacked Freeman's settlement, on the Loyalhanna creek, a few miles northeast of Hannastown, killed one of Freeman's sons and captured two of his daughters. At the same time a demonstration was made against the Brush creek settlement, to the westward, but the damage was confined to the killing of live stock and the burning of some farm buildings.[7]

At Hannastown a small force of militia was stationed by Colonel Edward Cook, the county lieutenant, and the settlers were advised to return and rebuild their houses. Only a few of them did so. Court was continued there for a few sessions and the owners of the property made an effort to retain the county seat. The General Assembly ordered the construction of a new road from Bedford to Pittsburg, and its course was located nearly three miles south of Hannastown, on the line of the present pike. This destroyed the last chance of the original county seat, and in January, 1787, the Westmoreland court began its sessions at Greensburg, on the new road.

At present Hannastown does not rise to the dignity of a village. Three or four houses and a blacksmith shop cluster at the cross roads, with a schoolhouse on the hill half a mile to the westward. Between the cross-roads and the schoolhouse the pioneer settlement lay, on what is now the farm of William Steel. The plow still turns up numerous bits of burned wood, and Mr. Steel has many little relics gathered from the fields. Among these is a ponderous iron key, which once unlocked the oaken door of Westmoreland county's log jail.

---

6 Pension petition of Mrs. Elizabeth Guthrie, formerly Mrs. Brownlee, made Feb. 5, 1829, published in Westmoreland Democrat, May 24, 1899; Frontier Forts, vol. ii., pp. 308, 324; Washington-Irvine Corr., p. 251.

7 Washington-Irvine Correspondence, p. 383.

CHAPTER XXVII.

THE ABANDONED EXPEDITION.

The Scots and other frontiersmen were far from being discouraged by their sad experience under Colonel Crawford. The fugitives from the Sandusky plain had barely returned to their homes, when they began to prepare for another campaign. A fierce determination possessed the borderers to crush the "red vipers" along the Sandusky river and arrangements were made to invade the Indian country once more as soon as the wheat and oats were harvested.

Brigadier General Irvine was asked to take the command and the principal men on the frontier agreed to furnish the provisions, not only for the volunteers, but for the regulars from Fort Pitt. The general agreed to lead the expedition if he should be satisfied with its size and equipment, and subscription papers were circulated for men, horses and food. Men of means who were too old for campaigning agreed to assist with horses and provisions.[1] The time for starting was first set for early in August, but the summer being dry and the grist mills without water, flour could not be ground and a postponement was announced until September 20.

General Irvine informed the Pennsylvania government of the preparation on the border, at the same time intimating that aid from the state and from Congress would be ac-

---
[1] Washington-Irvine Correspondence, pp. 123, 124, 175; Pennsylvania Archives, First Series, vol. ix., p. 576.

ceptable. A conference was held between members of the Pennsylvania Supreme Council and members of Congress, which resulted in a recommendation to General Washington, about the first of September, 1782, that the United States government should take part in a general campaign against the savages. At that time aggressive warfare had been suspended in the East and there was expectation of early peace with Great Britain. General Washington agreed that three expeditions should penetrate the Indian country, each to be composed of regulars, militia and volunteers, and Congress voted to bear the expenses of the regular contingents.

One expedition, to be commanded by Brigadier General Irvine, was to move from Fort Pitt against the Wyandots and Delawares on the Sandusky river; a second, under Major General James Potter, was to advance from Sunbury, Pa., into the Seneca land, in the Genesee valley, and a third was to be sent by the state of New York against the eastern Iroquois in the neighborhood of Oswego.[2]

Two companies of militia, one from York, and the other from Cumberland county, were sent to Westmoreland to guard its settlements while its own men were absent in the Indian country. Detachments of Colonel Moses Hazen's "Canadian regiment," stationed at Lancaster and Carlisle, were ordered to march to Fort Pitt and join General Irvine, who had at that post two companies of the Pennsylvania line under Captains Samuel Brady and John Clark.

General Lincoln, the Secretary at War, proposed that Irvine's force should aggregate 1,200 men, made up as follows: regulars from Ft. Pitt, 150; detachment from Hazen's regiment, 200; Pennsylvania rangers, 60; Pennsylvania and Virginia militia, 300; frontier volunteers, 490. The day for setting forth on the campaign, October 8, was fixed by General Lincoln, and Irvine was assured that by that time Hazen's regulars and the militia from the middle counties would be at Ft. Pitt. General Irvine immediately be-

---

[2] Washington-Irvine Correspondence, pp. 133, 134, 181, 183; Pennsylvania Archives, vol. ix., pp. 626, 630, 635, 636.

gan his arrangements for operations on an enlarged scale, but when October 8 came he found himself short of the promised reinforcements. On that day he wrote to the president of Pennsylvania that no rangers had appeared, that the few militiamen who had arrived were miserably furnished, and that he could not understand why Hazen's men had been detained. Still, he was determined to proceed if he could gather a force of 600 regulars and volunteers, and he had sent an officer (Captain Brady) along the road to hasten Hazen's detachment. He had again postponed the date until October 20.[3]

While preparations were making for this campaign the Indians came again against the border. At the beginning of September, 1782, Captain Andrew Bradt, with his company of 40 Canadian rangers and 238 Indians, Wyandots, Delawares and Shawnees, set out from Upper Sandusky to attack Wheeling. That settlement was defended by a stockade, called Fort Henry, which contained one swivel gun. The weapon was a useful relic. It had been thrown into the Ohio river by the French when they evacuated Fort Duquesne in 1758, and had been recovered by the pioneers. It had been made and brought to America for service against the British flag, but never fulfilled its mission until used on the fort at Wheeling. Within the stockade, when the approach of the enemy was discovered, all the inhabitants of the settlement took refuge. There were 27 men in the place, but only 18 were fit for duty. Colonel Ebenezer Zane, the pioneer settler, commanded the little garrison.

Captain Bradt's force crossed the Ohio and paraded before Fort Henry in the evening of Wednesday, September 11. The captain displayed the British flag and demanded a surrender. The demand was rejected, and soon afterward firing was opened at long range. At midnight the savages attempted to carry the stockade by storm, but were repulsed. The French swivel gun was used with good effect, as the Indians were very much afraid of any sort of a cannon. Two more futile assaults were made before day-

---

[3] Pennsylvania Archives, vol. ix., p. 648.

THE ABANDONED EXPEDITION. 185

light, and the besiegers then retired to a distance and kept up a steady firing during the day. Captain Bradt sent a negro to the fort with a second but unavailing demand for surrender, and during Thursday night a fourth desperate effort was made to storm the stockade. The brave riflemen again repulsed the savage horde, and shortly after dawn the discouraged assailants withdrew and recrossed the Ohio river. Among the fort's defenders one man had been wounded in the foot.[4]

After the failure at Wheeling about 70 of the Indians, anxious for scalps and plunder, cut loose from the main body of the marauders and went against the blockhouse of Abraham Rice on Buffalo creek, within the present township of Donegal, Washington county. From 2 o'clock in the afternoon of September 13 until 2 o'clock the following morning that blockhouse was successfully defended by only six men. They killed four of the Indians and lost one of their own number, George Felebaum, who was shot in the brain while peering through a loophole. The savages killed many cattle and burned a barn. On their return toward the Ohio river they met and killed two settlers who were going to Rice's relief. This was the last invasion of Western Pennsylvania by a large body of Indians.[5]

At Ft. Pitt General Irvine's preparations had been made and he was anxiously awaiting the arrival of Hazen's regulars, when, on October 23, he received from Philadelphia information that the Indian war was at an end and that his expedition was countermanded.[6]

The cessation of Indian depredations, which had been carried on with terrible results for six years, was the work of General Sir Guy Carleton, who had recently been appointed commander-in-chief of the British forces in America. He was a humane man, and had never approved the

---

[4] Washington-Irvine Correspondence, pp. 312, 397; Pennsylvania Archives, vol. ix., p. 638; Western Annals, p. 405.

[5] Western Annals, p. 406; Historical Collections of Pennsylvania, p. 661; Frontier Forts, vol. ii., pp. 404 to 410.

[6] Washington-Irvine Correspondence, p. 134.

employment of savages. Soon after his appointment to the supreme command he was shocked by the burning of Crawford and other American prisoners at Sandusky, and orders were conveyed to all British officers engaged on the border to exert their efforts to prevent further outrages by their red allies.

It is interesting to read the reply of Captain Alexander McKee, at that time a British agent among the Shawnees on the Great Miami and Mad rivers, to the letter which he received in regard to the Indian cruelties. "It is true," he wrote, "they have made sacrifices to their revenge after the massacre of their women and children, some being known to them to be perpetrators of it, but it was done in my absence or before I could reach any of the places to interfere. And I can assure you, sir, that there is not a white person here wanting in their duty to represent to the Indians in the strongest terms the highest abhorrence of such conduct, as well as the bad consequence that may attend it, to both them and us, being contrary to the rule of carrying on war by civilized nations."

General Carleton's protest against cruelties was soon followed by more radical action. He sent an order to the officers in command at Niagara and Detroit to cease entirely the sending out of Indian parties against the American frontiers and to act only on the defensive. This order reached DePeyster, at Detroit, late in August, and he at once sent couriers to the British officers at the Indian towns in Ohio to stop all incursions. The runner sent to Upper Sandusky reached there too late to stop Captain Bradt, who had already marched against Wheeling.

General Washington, in quarters at Newburg-on-the-Hudson, did not learn of General Carleton's action until September 23, when he immediately wrote to the authorities in Philadelphia to stop the expeditions at Sunbury and Fort Pitt.[7]

General Lincoln, on September 27, wrote to Generals

---

7 Washington-Irvine Correspondence, p. 135; Pennsylvania Archives, vol. ix., p. 641.

Hazen and Irvine that the expedition was off. The letter to Hazen reached that officer promptly and he returned with his command to Lancaster. The letter to Irvine was not sent by express rider, as it should have been, but was entrusted to some person traveling on private business. The bearer lingered by the way and was making little progress toward Ft. Pitt, when Captain Brady, riding in quest of Hazen's detachment, found the bearer of the letter at some wayside inn. Thus it was that the countermand reached General Irvine so late.[8]

The last stroke in the border war of the Revolution was inflicted by the Americans. While General Irvine was making ready to invade the Indian country from the eastward, General George Rogers Clark was preparing a similar movement from Kentucky. Correspondence passed between these officers for the purpose of securing simultaneous action. Clark's plan was to ascend the Great Miami and strike the Shawnee towns at the time when Irvine was operating against the Wyandots and Delawares. Early in October General Irvine sent a messenger down the Ohio river to Clark with the information that the Fort Pitt expedition would move on October 20, and Clark arranged to cross the Ohio from Kentucky at the same time. Washington's countermand held Irvine, but it was too late to stop Clark.

With 1,000 horsemen, General Clark crossed the Ohio at the site of Cincinnati, marched up the Great Miami and destroyed the two Shawnee towns of Lower and Upper Piqua, in what is now Miami county, Ohio. A detachment burned also the trading post of Peter Loramie and the adjacent Indian town, on the west branch of the Miami. The Indians had warning in time to hide the women and children in the woods, but they saved none of their property and the Kentuckians carried away a great quantity of plunder. Ten Indian scalps and seven prisoners were taken, while two of the Kentuckians were mortally wounded.

General Carleton's order concluded the Indian war of

---
8 Washington-Irvine Correspondence, pp. 134, 184.

the Revolution. That is, it ended the incursions of the savages as the allies of Great Britain, acting with British aid and under the direction of British officers, but it did not altogether stop the depredations of some of the Ohio savages acting on their own account. Small bands of Shawnees, seeking revenge for General Clark's work of destruction, invaded the settlements in the spring of 1783 and inflicted considerable injury. In the autumn of 1782, however, the sorely harried borderers were encouraged to believe that their distresses were at an end, and with earnestness they participated in the observance of the first general Thanksgiving Day celebrated in the United States on the last Thursday of November.[9]

---

[9] Pennsylvania Archives, vol. ix., p. 650.

CHAPTER XXVIII.

THE PEACE JOURNEY OF EPHRAIM DOUGLASS.

The residents of the frontier, in the opening of 1783, were happy in the expectation of peace, when they were startled and distressed by a series of Indian depredations. Several small parties of savages, in the latter part of March and the first week of April, invaded Westmoreland and Washington counties, struck severe blows and escaped quickly into the wilderness.

Four Indians appeared at a clearing in the valley of Brush creek, killed James Davis and his son in a field, took two other men captive and tried to break into the cabin, which was defended by a woman and an old man. One of the Indians tried to pry open the door with his gun, which he thrust in between the door and its frame. The man and the woman within seized the gun barrel and broke it loose from its stock, whereupon the Indians went away.[1]

In Washington county a man was killed within a mile of the new county seat on Chartiers creek, and a dozen persons were captured. Two of the prisoners, Mrs. Walker and a boy, regained their liberty, but the others were carried to the Shawnee towns on the headwaters of the Big Miami river.[2]

Some of the frontiersmen suspected that these raids were made by bands that had been out hunting all winter, and did not know of the peace made between Great Britain

---
1 Washington-Irvine Correspondence, p. 408; Pennsylvania Archives, vol. x., p. 22.
2 Pennsylvania Archives, vol. x., p. 167.

and the United States, or of the orders issued by the British commanders. Fear was felt that the Indians might keep up the war without British support, and appeals were sent to Philadelphia for peace treaties with the savage tribes. On April 4 the Pennsylvania Council asked Congress to take some action to pacify the Indians, and on April 29 the request was repeated, with the statement that 40 persons had been killed and captured, since spring opened, on the Pennsylvania frontiers.

Two days later Congress voted to send a messenger into the Indian country to inform the tribes that the King of Great Britain had been compelled to make peace with the United States; that the British had agreed to evacuate the forts at Detroit and Niagara, leaving the Indians to take care of themselves, and that the United States desired peace with the Indians, but were prepared for vigorous action if the tribes should prefer war. To execute this hard and dangerous mission the Secretary at War, Major General Benjamin Lincoln, chose Major Ephraim Douglass, of Pittsburg.[3]

Ephraim Douglass was the son of Adam Douglass, a Scot, and was born in Carlisle, in 1750. At the age of 18 he went to Fort Pitt, where he worked for a few years as a carpenter. He afterward engaged in the Indian trade at Pittsburg and Kittanning in partnership with Devereux Smith and Richard Butler.

In 1776 Douglass was appointed by Congress quartermaster of the Eighth Pennsylvania regiment. He was captured by the British at Bound Brook, N. J., on April 13, 1777, and for more than two years was a prisoner in New York. After his exchange, much broken in health, he was made the assistant commissary for the department of Fort Pitt. In the autumn of 1781 he was sent on a dangerous mission alone into the Indian country of Southern Ohio, and did not return until May, 1782. Major Douglass was a tall man, of great strength. His fearless-

---

[3] Washington-Irvine Correspondence, p. 188; Pennsylvania Archives, vol. x., pp. 45, 46.

ness, energy and persistence, added to his knowledge of the Indian country, recommended him to the Secretary at War.[4]

Douglass was accompanied on his journey by Captain George McCully, who had been associated with him in the Indian trade and had served with distinction in the Revolution, and by a wilderness guide. These three men, well mounted and carrying a white flag, left Fort Pitt on June 7, 1783, and rode to the Sandusky river, where they arrived on June 16.[5] They went to the principal town of the Delawares, where they were received with cordiality by Captain Pipe, the chief sachem. With him, for one reason and another, the messengers were compelled to remain for two weeks. The Indians were extremely punctilious in all matters of negotiations, either for peace or war, clinging to ancient forms with much solemn ceremony. While Captain Pipe declared himself to be strongly in favor of peace, he declined to enter into a council on the subject until after Major Douglass had treated with the Wyandots and the Shawnees. This was because the Wyandots and the Shawnees had taken up the hatchet first and had forced the Delawares into the war.

The chief of the Wyandots along the Sandusky river was Dunquat, the celebrated Half-King, and he was away at Detroit, but his wife thought that he would soon come home, and persuaded Douglass to wait for him. Captain Pipe was kind enough to send a runner to the Shawnee towns on the Big Miami, asking their chiefs to come to Sandusky to meet the American agent. In five days this runner returned with the news that the Shawnees had just been called to Detroit, to attend a great Indian council with the British commander there.

Pipe now advised Douglass to go to Detroit and meet all the Indian chiefs in the British presence. Dunquat did not return at the time his wife expected him, and Pipe said

---

4 Biographical sketch of Ephraim Douglass, in Veech's Monongahela of Old.
5 See the official report of Douglass to the Secretary at War, Pennsylvania Archives, vol. x., p. 83.

that even the Half-King could not make peace with the Americans without the authority of the Wyandot great council, which had its seat in Canada, near Detroit. Douglass, therefore, decided to go to the British fort, and on the last day of June he and McCully set forth, in company with Captain Pipe and two other Delawares. The time spent by Douglass at Sandusky had not been wasted. He had talked much with Pipe and other chiefs, and had influenced them to a friendly feeling toward the American states. He had likewise made a good impression among the old men and women in the Wyandot towns.

On the second day of their journey Douglass and his companions were met by Captain Matthew Elliott and three other persons, sent by Lieutenant Colonel DePeyster, the commander at Detroit, to conduct the Americans to the British post. This Elliott was one of the tories who had fled from Pittsburg in the spring of 1778, and he and Douglass had formerly been acquainted. Elliott carried a letter from DePeyster, inviting Douglass to attend the Indian council at Detroit.[6]

Douglass arrived at the British post on July 4 and had a very civil reception. DePeyster lodged him well and treated him kindly. Douglass soon learned, however, that the British commander would not permit him to hold a conference with the Indian chiefs.

DePeyster pleaded that he had no authority from his government to permit such a conference. He objected, moreover, to some of the language in Douglass's letter of instruction. It would never do to allow the Indians to be told that the King of England had been compelled to make peace. Such a statement might lead the tribes to feel a dangerous contempt for the British power. Neither was DePeyster willing that Douglass should tell the Indians that the British had agreed to evacuate Detroit. He had no knowledge that such an agreement had been made. He advised Douglass to go down to Niagara and state the terms

---

6 Pennsylvania Archives, vol. x., p. 62.

of his mission to Brigadier General Allan Maclean, who had greater authority in such affairs.

DePeyster did give material assistance to the object of Douglass's journey, by persuading the Indians to peace. On July 6 the great council was held in Fort Detroit. It was attended by the chiefs of 11 tribes, representing nearly all the Indians from the Scioto river to Lake Superior.[7] To them DePeyster made a long talk, conveying the essential part of Douglass's message. He told the chiefs of the peace between Great Britain and the United States, and that he could no longer give them help in their war against the Americans. He announced that the Americans desired peace with the Indian tribes, and had sent Major Douglass to invite them to a treaty, and he advised all the Indians to cease their warfare against the United States.

This address had a good effect on the assembled savages, and although they could hold no council with the American envoy, they surrounded his lodging and saluted him with pronounced expressions of friendship. On the day after the council Douglass and McCully left Detroit and traveled overland, through Ontario, toward Niagara. At that British post, which they reached in four days, General Maclean raised the same objections as those offered by Lieutenant Colonel DePeyster. He would not permit Major Douglass to speak directly to the Iroquois chiefs, but on his own account and through Colonel Butler, the Indian superintendent, he informed the chiefs of the desires of the United States for peace with all the tribes.

While at Fort Niagara, Douglass had a long private conversation with Joseph Brant, the celebrated war chief of the Mohawks, and did what he could to persuade Brant of the kindly intentions of the Americans toward the Indians.

General Maclean urged Douglass to go to Quebec and confer with the governor general of Canada, but the major felt that he had fulfilled, as far as possible, the duties of his

---

[7] Chippewas, Ottawas, Wyandots, Shawnees, Delawares, Kickapoos, Weas, Miamis, Pottawattamies, Piankeshaws and a few Senecas.

mission, and desired to return to the states. General Maclean sent him by boat to Oswego, whence Douglass journeyed, by way of Albany, to Princeton, N. J., where the federal government was then located, and made his report to General Lincoln.

This mission of Douglass effected complete peace on the frontiers. To his efforts were due the cessation of the Indian War of the Revolution on the borders of New York, Pennsylvania and Virginia.

[The End.]

INDEX.

Amberson, William, Pittsburg merchant, 111.
Anderson, Isaac, soldier, 145.
Armstrong, Ft., at Kittanning, 96, 103, 110.
Armstrong, John. soldier, 53, 96.
Association of Westmoreland county, 15, 25.
Bald Eagle, Delaware chief, 71, 94.
Ballantine, Alexander, 48.
Bane, Joseph, 164.
Barr, Ft., in Derry settlement, 117, 119, 121.
Barr, Robert, 116, 117, 119, 121.
Bayard, Stephen, officer of the Revolution, 65, 96.
Beaver river, 42, 80.
Bedford county, 40, 49-53.
Beelor, Joseph, lieutenant of Yohogania county, Va., 113.
Beeson, John, 164.
Beloved, Delaware war chief (See Wingenund).
Benham, Robert, 55, 58.
Big Cat, Delaware chief, 124, 153, 160.
Biggs, John, militia officer, 164, 169.
Big Runaway on the Susquehanna, 68.
Bilderback, Charles, militia officer, 157, 164.
Bird, Henry, British officer, 84, 85.
Blacklick creek, 26, 116, 118.
Blaine, Ephraim, merchant and army contractor, 62.
Boundary dispute between Pennsylvania and Virginia, 6, 7, 24, 110, 113, 132, 135.
Boyd, John, 62.
Braddock road. 6, 8.
Bradt, Andrew, British officer, 184, 185, 186.
Brady, James, brother of Samuel, killed by Indians, 70.
Brady, John, officer of the Revolution, 70, 90.

Brady, Samuel, soldier and scout, 65, 70, 71, 89-94, 96, 106-108, 112-113, 183, 184, 187.
Brant, Joseph, Mohawk war chief, 144, 193.
Brinton, John, 164.
Brodhead, Daniel, officer of the Revolution, 68, 79, 83, 90,102, 105, 109, 110-114, 132, 149; colonel of the Eighth Pennsylvania, 65, 66; commander of the Western Department, 86, 88; expedition against the Senecas, 95-101; expedition against the Delawares, 123-130; relieved of his command, 147.
Brokenstraw creek, 97, 99.
Brown, Basil, 55, 58-59.
Brown, Thomas, 55.
Brownlee, Joseph, killed by Indians, 180.
Brownsville, 55.
Bruce, William, 164.
Brush creek, 8, 170, 173, 181, 189.
Buckaloons, Indian town on Allegheny river, 97.
Buckongahelas, Delaware war chief, 126.
Butler, John, tory leader in New York, 19, 92, 177.
Butler, Richard, trader and soldier, 19, 26, 62, 65, 69, 190.
Caldwell, William, British officer, 165, 166.
Cambray, Chevalier de, military engineer, 81, 82.
Campbell, Charles, militia officer, 116, 118.
Campbell, John, trader and land owner, 10, 79.
Campbell, William, 139.
Canon, John, founder of Canonsburg, 14, 135.
Carleton, Sir Guy, British general, 185, 186.
Carnaghan, John, Militia officer, 15.
Carnaghan's blockhouse, 29, 140.

(195)

Carpenter, John, his capture by Indians, 154.
Carson, Moses, 62, 69.
Cavet, James, leader on the frontier, 10, 11.
Chartiers settlement, 6, 107, 112, 160.
Cherry, Ft., on Little Raccoon creek, 151.
Cherry, John, his death, 151, 152.
Chestnut Ridge, 8.
Chilloway, Job, Delaware Indian and interpreter, 75.
Clark, George Rogers, famous American officer, 35, 54, 95, 131-138, 141, 187.
Clark, John, American officer, 83, 183.
Collie, Isaac, 55.
Conemaugh river, 8, 116, 119.
Conewango creek, 97, 99.
Connolly, John, Dunmore's agent at Pittsburg, 7, 10, 13, 14, 16, 24.
Cook, Edward, frontier leader and magistrate, 10, 14; lieutenant of Westmoreland county, 146, 164, 181.
Corbly, John, Rev., massacre of his family, 164.
Cornplanter, Seneca chief, 71, 95, 98, 99.
Cornstalk, Shawnee war chief, 20, 23,
Coshocton, chief town of the Delawares, 21, 47, 81, 82; destroyed by Brodhead, April, 1781, 123-130.
Cox, Gabriel, militia officer, 135, 136.
Cracraft, Charles, American officer, 142.
Craig, Isaac, artillery officer, 132, 137.
Craig, Samuel, militia officer, 16, 116, 118.
Craig, Samuel, Jr., 145.
Crawford, Ft., on the Allegheny river, 88, 103, 110.
Crawford, John, son of Colonel William, 167, 168.
Crawford, Valentine, brother of William, 12.

Crawford, William, surveyor and American officer, 10, 12, 14, 27, 29, 35, 41, 48, 66, 79, 88, 132; his capture and death at the stake, 164-168.
Crawford, William, son of Valentine, 167, 168.
Croghan, George, trader, Indian agent and land owner, 10, 13, 14.
Cuyahoga river, 41.
Delaware Indians, 18, 20, 23, 47, 73, 81, 82, 96, 106, 149, 156, 167, 170, 184, 191; alliance with the United States, 74-79, 114, 123; joined the hostile league, 124; driven from the Muskingum, 130.
DePeyster, Arent Schuyler, British commander at Detroit, 126, 129, 144, 149, 150, 186, 192, 193.
Derry settlement, 8, 116.
Detroit, British headquarters in the west, 20, 22, 73, 126, 131, 133, 144, 149, 165, 190, 192, 193.
Doddridge, Joseph, pioneer historian, 128.
Douglass, Ephraim, trader and soldier, 62, 190-194.
Douglass, John, magistrate, 136.
Downing, Timothy, 164.
Dunmore, John Murray, Earl of, 7, 16, 32.
Dunmore's war, 11, 12.
Dunquat, Wyandot halfking, 21, 149, 151, 191.
Eighth Regiment of the Pennsylvania Line, organization, 25, 62, 190; march to the East, 26, 63, 64; return to the border, 60, 67-72; services on the frontier, 80, 83, 86.
Elliott, Matthew, renegade and British officer, 46, 57, 149, 168, 192.
Fayette City, 32, 147.
Fife, William, 164.
Findley, George, 116.
Fink, John, 154.
Finley, Ebenezer, son of Rev. James, 120.

INDEX.

Finley, James, Rev., pioneer preacher, 120.
Finley, John, soldier, 69, 79.
Finley, Joseph L., soldier, 79.
Fleming, Richard, 144.
Food, scarcity of on the frontier, 103, 109-113, 115.
Forbes road, 6, 8.
Fowler, Alexander, merchant, 147.
Franklin, Benjamin, 18.
French creek, 100.
Gaddis, Thomas, 164.
Gibson, George, trader and soldier, 32-36.
Gibson, John, trader and soldier, 14, 19, 32, 66, 77, 79, 147, 160; in command at Ft. Laurens, 83-86.
Girty, George, brother of Simon, 144.
Girty, James, brother of Simon, 47.
Girty, Simon, interpreter and tory, 20, 57, 129; flight from Ft. Pitt, 46; at siege of Ft. Laurens, 83-85; at the torture of Crawford, 168.
Gnadenhuetten, Moravian Indian town on the Tuscarawas, 125, 150; massacre of March, 1782, 153-161.
Graham, Arthur, soldier, 79.
Greensburg, 176, 181.
Guthrie, William, 116.
Guyasuta (Big Cross), Seneca chief, 18, 95, 98, 177.
Half-king of the Wyandots (see Dunquat).
Hamilton, Henry, British commander at Detroit, 22, 39, 44, 47, 49, 95.
Hand, Edward, American general, 17, 37-43, 45, 48, 60.
Hand, Ft., in Northern Westmoreland, 88, 90.
Hanna, Robert, tavern keeper and magistrate, 7, 10, 11, 176; capture of his wife and daughter, 180.
Hannastown, county seat of Westmoreland, 7, 24, 72, 103, 114; patriotic meetings there, 11, 14; destruction by Indians, July 13, 1782, 176.
Hardin, John, 136.

Hardin, John, Jr., American officer, 89, 98, 136, 164.
Hardman, head chief of the Shawnees, 20.
Harrison, Lawrence, American officer, 33, 88.
Harrison, William, 167, 168.
Hays, Christopher, Westmoreland leader and legislator, 10, 134, 137, 146.
Hazen, Moses, American officer, 183, 187.
Heath, Andrew, 55.
Heckewelder, John, Moravian missionary, 124, 125, 149.
Henry, Ft., at Wheeling, 34, 88, 125, 141, 184.
Henry, Patrick, governor of Virginia, 18, 54.
Hinkston, John, Indian fighter, 119.
Hoagland, John, 164, 169.
Hood, Andrew, 164.
Hopkins, Captain, 119.
Huffnagle, Michael, 10, 62, 178.
Huntingdon, 51.
Huron Indians (see Wyandots).
Indian treaties, at Ft. Pitt, October, 1775, 18; at Ft. Pitt, October, 1776, 23; at Ft. Pitt, September, 1778, 74-79.
Iroquois Indians, 5, 18, 19, 28, 52, 68, 90, 144, 193.
Irvine, William, American general, 97 (note), 147, 153, 160, 163, 164, 172, 173, 182, 185, 187.
Jack, John, scout, 151.
Jack, Matthew, soldier, 178.
Jack, William, soldier and magistrate, 90.
Jackson, Philip, 151.
Johnson, Sir Guy, British Indian agent, 19.
Jones, David, Rev., missionary to the Indians, 9.
Killbuck, Delaware chief, 21, 75, 79, 123, 124, 125, 126, 130, 153, 160.
Killgore, David, American officer, 62.
King's Orchard, at Pittsburg, 45.
Kiskiminetas river, 26, 29, 103, 119.

Kittanning, 5, 25, 29, 51, 63, 96, 119.
Knight, John, military surgeon, 163, 167, 168.
Knotts, John, 58.
Kuskuskee, Indian town on Beaver river, 97 (note), 107.
Lame Indian, story of, 170.
Lanctot, Godfrey, 106.
Laughlin, Randall, 118.
Laurel Hill, 6.
Laurens, Ft., on the Tuscarawas, 82-87, 96.
Leet, Daniel, 135, 164.
Leet, William, 164.
Lewis, Andrew, American officer, 74-79.
Lewis, Thomas, brother of Andrew, 74.
Leyba, Francisco de, Spanish commandant at St. Louis, 56.
Licking river, scene of Rodgers's defeat, 56-59.
Ligonier, 8, 41, 90, 106.
Lincoln, Benjamin, secretary at war, 183, 186, 190, 194.
Linn, William, 32-36.
Lochry, Archibald, 10, 146; lieutenant-colonel of associators, 15; lieutenant of Westmoreland, 40, 102, 122, 134, 138, 146; fatal voyage down the Ohio, 139-145.
Long, Peter, hunter and scout, 20.
Loskiel, George Henry, Moravian missionary and historian, 158.
Loyalhanna creek, 8, 116, 181.
McCleery, William, militia officer, 113.
McClelland, John, militia officer, 134, 164, 169.
McClure, David, Rev., 62.
McCulloch, John, 14.
McCully, George, 191, 192.
McElroy, Patrick, 55.
McFarlane, Andrew, capture by Indians, 24.
McFarlane, James, 24, 29.
McGeehan, Duncan, 164.
McIntosh, Ft., at mouth of Beaver river, 80-81, 87.
McIntosh, Lachlan, American general, 60, 67, 73, 79, 80-86.

Mackay, Eneas, magistrate and American officer, 10, 24, 26, 62, 64.
McKee, Alexander, 45, 186; flight from Pittsburg, 46.
McKee's Rocks, 45.
Maclean, Allan, British officer, 193.
Mahoning river, tributary of the Allegheny, 93, 96.
Mahoning river, tributary of the Beaver, 42.
Mann, Andrew, 63.
Markle, Gaspard, 140.
Marshel, James, lieutenant of Washington county, 135, 136, 155, 164.
Mason and Dixon's line, 7.
Miami Indians, 33, 83, 84.
Miami river, 141, 186, 187.
Miller, John, 164.
Miller, Samuel, 62, 180; killed by Indians, 72.
Mills, Benjamin, 79.
Mingo Bottom, on Ohio river, 155, 160, 164, 167.
Mingo Indians, Iroquois living in Ohio, 18, 21, 23, 24, 83, 84.
Money depreciation, 109.
Monongahela river, 8, 32, 110, 113, 132, 135, 141.
Monongalia county, Va., 35 (note), 80, 113, 132.
Montour, John, French-Iroquois, 21, 23, 124, 125.
Moorhead, Samuel, border leader, 26, 29, 90.
Moravian missions, 124, 125, 153; driven from the Tuscarawas, 148-151; massacre at Gnadenhuetten, 155-160.
Morgan, Daniel, American general, 65.
Morgan, George, merchant and Indian agent, 20, 23, 74, 77 (note).
Morgan's Rifle Corps, 65.
Mountz, Providence, 15.
Muncy Indians, a clan of the Delawares, 42, 71, 89, 94, 100, 104, 105.
Munn, James, 164.
Muskingum river, 20, 126.
Myers, Eliezer, soldier, 63.

Nanowland, Delaware warrior, 91, 93, 99, 124, 125, 153, 160.
Neville, John, Virginia officer, 16, 37, 38.
Newcomer, chief sachem of the Delawares, 21, 47.
Newcomer's Town, 127.
New Orleans, 33, 56.
Nicholson, Joseph, interpreter and guide, 20, 21, 99.
Nicholson, Thomas, 164.
Nimwha, Shawnee chief, 76.
Ohio county, Va., 35, 80, 125, 132.
Ohio river, 33, 56, 137, 141.
Oil creek, 100.
Olentangy, Battle at, 167.
Ormsby, John, 10.
Orr, Robert, 139, 144, 145.
Ourry, Wendel, 62.
Palmer's Fort, Ligonier valley, 41.
Pentecost, Dorsey, surveyor and magistrate, 10, 132, 135.
Perry, James, 92.
Piggott, James, 62.
Pipe, Delaware chief, 47, 75, 79, 124, 126, 149, 191.
Pittsburg, 9, 13; character of its population, 8, 9; patriotic meeting there, 13; occupied by Virginia troops, 16-17; transferred to continental care, 37; tory plots, 44.
Pluggy, Mohawk warrior, 21.
Pluggystown, Mingo village on Scioto, 21, 24.
Poe, Adam, 151, 152.
Poe, Andrew, 151, 152.
Pollock, Oliver, merchant at New Orleans, 33, 54.
Pomeroy, John, militia officer, 116, 117, 121.
Powder, procured from the Spaniards, 31-35, 54-56.
Proctor, John, pioneer leader, 10, 15.
Quoshquoshink, Delaware town on the Allegheny, 97.
Raccoon creek, 104, 154.
Randolph, Ft., at Point Pleasant, 40, 88.
Rankin, Thomas, 164.
Rattlesnake flag, 16.
Red Bank creek, 71, 93.

Redstone, 45, 54, 55, 136.
Reed, David, 164.
Reed, Ft., at Hannastown, 176.
Reed, Joseph, President of Pennsylvania, 133, 134, 146.
Rice's blockhouse, 185.
Ritchie, Craig, 164.
Roads of Western Pennsylvania, 6, 8, 181.
Rodgers, David, his defeat and death at Licking river, 14, 54-58.
Rose, John, (Henri-Gustave Rosenthal), Russian volunteer in America, 163, 164, 167.
Ross, Ezekiel, 164.
Russell, William, Virginia officer, 66.
Saint Clair, Arthur, American officer, 8, 10, 15, 16.
Salem, Moravian Indian town on the Tuscarawas, 124, 150, 157, 158, 160.
Sandusky plain, battle of, 166.
Sandusky river, 21, 104, 106, 130, 148, 150, 156, 165, 191.
Sandusky, Upper, 107, 129, 152, 165, 168, 184.
Scalps, rewards for, 106.
Schoenbrun (Beautiful Well), Moravian Indian town, 150, 159, 160, 165.
Scioto river, 20, 104, 141.
Scotosh, Wyandot chief, son of the Half-King, 151, 152.
Scott, Thomas, frontier leader, 137, 146.
Semple, Samuel, tavern keeper at Pittsburg, 14.
Seneca Indians, 18, 39, 71, 89, 95-100, 104, 106, 177.
Seventh Virginia Regiment, 163.
Sewickley settlement, 8, 10, 92, 134, 140.
Shannon, Samuel, militia officer, 139, 142.
Shawnee Indians, 11, 12, 18, 20, 23, 33, 39, 46, 47, 75, 77, 95, 104, 144, 166, 168, 184, 186, 187, 189.
Shepherd, David, lieutenant of Ohio county, Va., 35, 125.
Shields, John, 15, 116, 117.

Sinking Spring valley, 50.
Slaves in Western Pennsylvania, 8, 146.
Slippery Rock creek, 101.
Slover, John, guide, 164, 168.
Smith, Devereux, 10, 24, 190.
Smith, James, pioneer and soldier, 15, 41, 119.
Smoky Island, at Pittsburg, 130, 153, 160.
Snow, the deep, 102.
Speer, Joseph, trader, 25.
Springer, Uriah, soldier, 112.
Squaw campaign of General Hand, 37-43.
Stephenson, John, 79.
Stokely, Thomas, soldier, 139, 144.
Stoops, Mrs. Jennie, 107.
Surphlit, Robert, tory, 46.
Swearingen, Van, border leader and soldier, 19, 62, 63, 65, 89.
Thanksgiving day, 188.
Thirteenth Virginia regiment, 35, 38, 48, 66, 67, 80, 83.
Tionesta river, 97.
Tomlinson's run, 151.
Tories, at Pittsburg, 44-48; in Bedford county, 49.
Turney, John, British officer, 165.
Turtle creek, 8, 106, 172.
Tuscarawas river, 81, 124, 127, 148-150, 153, 157.
Upper Sandusky (see Sandusky).
Venango trail, 100.
Veness, Jerome, 71.
Vernon, Frederick, American officer, 86, 87.
Walhonding river, 21, 150, 151.
Wallace, Ft., near the Kiskiminetas, 41, 117, 119-121.
Wallace, Richard, of Ft. Wallace, 116, 117, 144.
Wallace, Robert, of Raccoon creek, 155, 158; capture of his family, 154.
Walthour's blockhouse, 163, 170.
Ward, Edward, prominent resident of Pittsburg, 14.
Washington county, 8, 135, 151.

Washington, George, his connection with frontier operations, 9, 12, 37, 43, 60, 61, 86, 95, 101, 132, 147, 183, 186.
Washnash, Muncy war chief, 105.
West Augusta, District of, 13, 14, 35 (note).
Westmoreland county, erection and extent, 5; character of its settlers, 6, 8-10; patriotic organizations, 11, 14; military bodies, 14, 15, 62, 63, 105, 139; Col. Lochry's expedition and disaster, 139; destruction of Hannastown, 176.
Weston, John, Bedford tory, 50-52.
Weston, Richard, 50, 53.
Wheeling, 34, 40, 125, 127, 137, 141, 184.
White Eyes, Delaware chief sachem, 18, 21, 23, 47, 74-79, 124; his death, 82.
Willard, ——, killed by the Indians, 163, 170, 171.
Williamson, David, militia officer, 153; raid on Gnadenhuetten, 155-161; in Crawford's expedition, 164, 167.
Wilson, George, magistrate and soldier, 10, 26, 62, 64.
Wilson, James, leader of the Derry settlement, 116, 117, 119, 121.
Wilson, William, trader, 20-23.
Wingenund, Delaware chief, 76, 126.
Wolf clan of the Delawares (See Muncy Indians).
Wyandot Indians, 18, 20, 22, 23, 29, 83, 104, 106, 111, 112, 129, 144, 149, 151, 156, 165, 184, 191.
Wyoming, massacre of, 68.
Yohogania county, Va., 35 (note), 80, 113, 132.
Youghiogheny river, 8, 141.
Zane, Ebenezer, Wheeling pioneer, 185.
Zane, Jonathan, scout and guide, 99, 164.
Zeisberger, David, Moravian missionary, 97 (note), 149.

www.ingramcontent.com/pod-product-compliance
Lightning Source LLC
Chambersburg PA
CBHW071417160426
43195CB00013B/1728